MAUREEN McTEER

RESIDENCES
Homes of Canada's Leaders

Foreword: Pierre Berton   Photography: Ted Grant

Prentice-Hall Canada Inc., Scarborough, Ontario

Acknowledgments

No book that attempts to record history, on whatever scale, is an individual effort. During the five years this project was being researched, some two hundred people were contacted personally by letter or telephone. Of that number, I interviewed at least half. It was an adventure for me to dig out the treasures that lay hidden in boxes in private homes, in libraries and in the Public Archives of Canada. But more important, it was an honour to have so many people share their memories with me.

While every one of those people made a unique contribution to this book, I would be remiss not to mention with special gratitude Mrs. Diana Rowley, Mr. Cyril Currier, Mrs. Mary Edwards, Mr Angus Wilson, Mrs. Carolyn Weir, Mr. Robert Major, Mrs. Jean Wright, Mrs Rita McConkey and Mr. Stanley Healey.

For their untiring professional assistance, I offer my sincere thanks to Louise Roy at the City of Ottawa Archives, to Glen Wright at the Public Archives of Canada, and to the staff at the Diefenbaker Centre in Saskatoon. For their advice and patience in typing and retyping the manuscript, thanks also go to Jean Bye and Michèle Villeneuve.

Finally, there are those without whose invaluable assistance and guidance this book would never have become a reality. Special thanks go to my agent Lucinda Vardey and editor Janice Whitford at Prentice-Hall for coordinating the publication, and to Linda Findlay for editing and guiding the project through production.

Canadian Cataloguing in Publication Data

McTeer, Maureen, 1952-
    Residences: Homes of Canada's Leaders

ISBN 0-13-774539-7

1. Prime Ministers–Canada–Homes.   2. Stornoway (Ottawa, Ont.)
3. Historic buildings–Ontario–Ottawa region.
I. Grant, Ted, 1929-   II. Title

FC3096.7.M37   971.3′84   C82-094776-8
F1059.5.09M37

Prentice-Hall, Inc., Englewood Cliffs, New Jersey
Prentice-Hall International, Inc., London
Prentice-Hall of Australia, Pty., Ltd., Sydney
Prentice-Hall of India, Pvt., Ltd., New Delhi
Prentice-Hall of Japan, Inc., Tokyo
Prentice-Hall of Southeast Asia (Pte.), Ltd., Singapore
Prentice-Hall do Brazil Ltda., Rio de Janeiro

Production Editor: Linda Findlay
Designer: René Demers
Production: Jan Cheesman
Composition: CompuScreen Typesetting Ltd.
Cover Photograph: Mia & Klaus
End paper Photograph: Ted Grant

ISBN 0-13-774539-7

Printed in Canada by The Bryant Press Limited

Contents

Foreword

Halfway through this intriguing study of Canada's three official residences, I was struck by an obvious realization. Maureen McTeer is one of the few living Canadians – a tiny handful – properly equipped to write this book.

Apart from Maryon Pearson, Pierre and Margaret Trudeau, and her own husband, she is the only living Canadian to have occupied all three residences. Thus she brings a special intimacy to her descriptions and an inner knowledge of each home that enhances the value of the work.

She has, of course, done more than this. Every house has a story; but these houses, by their nature and their years, have many. Ms. McTeer has not only dug into the past of all three, she has also taken the trouble to interview several of the former owners. The results are often surprising.

Thus, this is more than a picture book for the curious. It is a longtime historical resource and not just for the academics. It is well within the bounds of possibility that some future Canadian novelist, searching for an authentic domestic background for a fictional prime minister, will find this book an irreplaceable research tool.

There are two other points to be made. First, in choosing these three official residences for its leading public servants, the Canadian government did not take the obvious but expensive step of building brand new "modern" edifices. Instead, it recycled what was already in place at a fraction of the cost, and, as Ms. McTeer so clearly shows, to the benefit of the future occupants. Does anybody believe that a modern building, designed by the Department of Public Works, would have been an improvement on any of these?

Second, these three buildings – each with a history and each magnificent in its own way – would certainly have been destroyed in the name of "progress" had a use not been found for them.

Therein lies a lesson for the nation. We have to learn to halt the senseless waste of our building stock – for practical economic reasons as well as for sentimental heritage reasons. I am happy that the case for this new and growing attitude is made implicitly in the pages that follow.

Pierre Berton
Chairman of the Board
The Heritage Canada Foundation

Preface

Old houses have always charmed me. Even when I was a child it did not satisfy me simply to know who built the houses of my family, friends and neighbours; I wanted to know the story of the people who had lived in them. To me, each house had a mood, a character – happy or haunted or lonely, depending on the people who were living or had lived there. The architecture attracted my eye, but the history stimulated my imagination.

In 1976, when we first moved into Stornoway, the official home of Canada's Leader of the Opposition, I was amazed to learn then that only a handful of people knew anything about the history of the house. I resolved at that time to do something about it. But it took four years and two moves before I could find time to do the research required to complete this book. By then my project had grown in scope to include the Prime Minister's permanent and country residences. I had also enlisted the help of my good friend, Ted Grant, who agreed to handle the photography. Now Canadians who have never seen the interiors of these three official residences will be given a glimpse of their beauty.

I have tried to capture for the reader a history that is, at its heart, the story of the people who have lived in three of Canada's official residences. It was not always easy to reconstruct what took place in the past. I do hope, though, that those who gave their time so generously during the writing of this book will feel that my presentation of their stories does them justice.

Have you ever stood outside a house and wondered about the generations of people who have lived there? Were they happy? Were they prosperous? Were their children healthy? Were there any secrets hidden within the walls of their homes?

As someone who had always been fascinated by old homes, I pondered these questions and many more that hot June morning in 1979, as I stood at the door of 24 Sussex Drive waiting impatiently for someone to answer my ring. Now that my husband had become Prime Minister of Canada, this house was to be our home. What was the history of this magnificent place? Someone had called it "Gorffwysfa", but what did that mean?

The imposing front door, flanked by the bottom half of the Canadian Coat of Arms chiseled in stone and by two members of the RCMP, indicated that it was an official residence. But how had it come to be used for such a purpose, and what of the people who had lived there before?

A woman dressed in a maid's uniform answered the door, interrupting my daydream. Quietly, my curiosity piqued, I walked for the first time into the main hall of 24 Sussex Drive. As I toured our future home, I became determined to discover and to share with Canadians some of its history.

24 SUSSEX DRIVE
Home of Canada's Prime Minister

The Past

While researching the history of the house at 24 Sussex Drive, I discovered that it was really a reflection of Ottawa's history and the people who made it.

Before Canada became a nation, Bytown, later rechristened Ottawa and made the capital city, was a major lumbering centre. In the early nineteenth century, when Napoleon's Baltic blockade cut Britain off from Scandinavian sources of timber for her fleet, the mother country turned to her colonies for supplies. Situated where the Rideau Canal joined the Ottawa River, Bytown was in a good position to take advantage of the booming lumber business, and the Ottawa Valley became one of Britain's prime sources of lumber.

THE CURRIERS

Drawn to this fast-growing forest frontier, Joseph Merrill Currier, the youngest of seven sons, arrived at Buckingham, Quebec in 1837, at the age of 17, from North Troy, Vermont. He was intent on carving out a future for himself in the lumber industry in this northern land. Immediately, he became involved in the lumber trade with a well-known local lumber merchant named James Maclaren. Shortly after, he married Christina Stenhouse Wilson, and worked for the next decade on establishing himself and making his fortune in the lumber business. Some twelve years later, in 1853, seeking a new challenge, he sold his interests in Buckingham, and moved with his wife and two small children to New Edinburgh, a small but prospering lumber town located one mile from Ottawa. There, he rented the lumber mill at the Rideau Falls, which, up until that time, was owned by Thomas MacKay. Later, he went into partnership with Moss Kent Dickinson, a prominent Bytown businessman, and later Mayor of Ottawa between 1864 and 1866. With the passing years, Joseph Currier's prosperity grew apace with that of Ottawa (Bytown's new name, on being incorporated as a city in 1855). By 1855, two more Currier children had been born and the family continued to enjoy the social and political prominence that came with personal wealth and position in their community. Joseph and Christina were happy, and took much pleasure in their four healthy, young children.

But this was the Ottawa of the mid-nineteenth century, where innoculation against disease was rare and infant mortality was appallingly high. In September 1855, tragedy struck the Currier family. Within ten days, three of their small children died of scarlet fever. Only six-year-old James was spared. Christina, beautiful and sensitive, would not be consoled. For three years, her devoted husband, family and friends tried to bring her back to the living. But on July 18, 1858, she died.

An early topographical map of the MacKay Estate, much of which later became the section of Ottawa known as New Edinburgh.

Left alone, Joseph turned his attention to the raising of his young son, James, and to the affairs of his business. James attended the Ottawa Grammar school and was later sent to the Riverview Military College in Poughkeepsie, New York.

In 1857, Joseph had joined with his partner, Moss Kent Dickinson, to build a flour mill in the present-day town of Manotick, Ontario. Situated about sixteen miles south of Parliament Hill, and officially opened on February ll, 1860, the mill was powered by special water turbines – a model of new technology.

At about the same time, Joseph met a beautiful young woman named Anna Crosby. Although there was an age difference of twenty-one years, the romance flourished under the strict eyes of her parents and chaperones. On Anna's twentieth birthday, her parents consented to her engagement and, on January 29, 1861, the wedding took place at Lake George, New York.

Joseph had been working very hard at the new mill, so the couple decided to take an extended honeymoon in New York state. They went away for the entire month of February, and then returned to their home in Manotick.

In early March of 1861, Joseph and Moss Kent Dickinson organized a day of festivities to celebrate the first anniversary of the mill. Part of the day's activities included a tour of inspection of the mill itself, and the Curriers decided to lead the way for all their guests. A smiling Anna, elegantly dressed and coiffed in the fashion of the day proudly took her new husband's arm and strolled through the building. All the machines were turned on to show friends and officials alike the power of the water turbines. No one could speak above the noise, and all marvelled at the mill's technology and delighted in its obvious success.

Then suddenly, as if out of a nightmare, Anna lost her balance. She fought to keep a hold on her husband's arm, but her billowing crinoline was caught in one of the machines. Her friends and guests, standing only a few feet away, were powerless to help. Her screams were barely audible above the noise, and as her husband and guests watched in shocked horror, Anna was sucked into the machine, hurled against its post, and killed before the machine could be stopped.

Joseph had lost his first wife and three of their four children. Now, less than two months after their wedding, Anna had been lost to him as well. Alone again and unable to bear living near the mill, he withdrew from his partnership with Moss Kent Dickinson and returned to New Edinburgh.

Partly to alleviate his grief, Joseph's friends encouraged him to continue to play an active role in all aspects of the growing community in and around Ottawa. His business interests were expanding and, after considerable encouragement, he decided to try his hand at politics. In 1863, he was elected to the Ontario legislature for the first time; and in 1867, as a new nation was being born, he sought and won the right to represent the riding of Ottawa in the first Dominion Parliament.

By 1867, Ottawa was becoming more than an industrial and manufacturing centre: it was also becoming the political and social focus of the nation.

People from abroad, involved in both business and government, frequently sailed into Canada via the St. Lawrence to Montreal and then on to Ottawa. As one of the city's leading citizens, Joseph Currier was often present at social gatherings to honour or entertain these distinguished guests. It was at one of these soirées that he met Hannah Wright, who was to become his third wife.

The granddaughter of Philemon Wright, the founder of Hull, Quebec, Hannah had moved in very wealthy circles and had made a reputation for herself as one of the most charming and accomplished hostesses in the capital city. She loved to entertain in grand style, and when Joseph proposed marriage to her, he offered to build her the house of her dreams as his personal wedding gift.

The flour mill at Manotick, Ontario, which J.M. Currier built in 1860 with his partner, M.K. Dickinson.

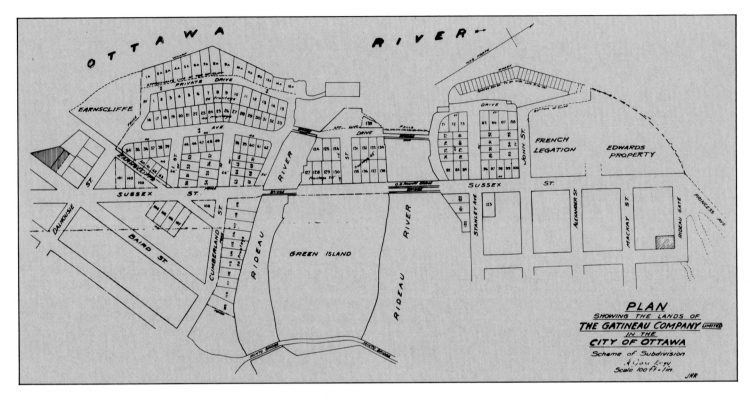

He put but two conditions on his gift: they would live near the water and the forests that had helped make his fortune, and, in an attempt to find peace at last, he would call their home "Gorffwysfa", the Welsh word for "place of peace".

In May of 1866, construction began on the house that was to become one of our most important historical residences. The following newspaper report on its progress appeared in the *Ottawa Citizen* on November 1, 1867:

A map of the properties around Sussex Street in the early twentieth century. The Edwards property is near the top right-hand corner.

It is built of dark grey stones, faced with Gloucester limestone and roofed with tin. The style of the building is Gothic and the design chaste and elegant. The mantlepieces are of marble. The wood-work is of the best possible material and quality; the floors being walnut, butternut and pine, the boards about three inches wide; the stairs are oak, and the doors and windows ash, butternut and walnut. In the ceiling, between the joists, a composition of mortar is placed to deafen sounds from above. The building is heated with hot air and furnished with hot and cold water baths. The plastering is done in the best style of the art, with rich cornicing and ornamental work in every room . . . Mr. Currier's brother, Mr. J.M. Currier, of Springfield, Massachusetts, was the architect. The dimensions of the building are 82 X 40 feet, and the cost will probably exceed $15,000.

Contiguous to the house are appropriate outhouses, including a lodge, wood-house, conservatory and summerhouse.

Log booms below 24 Sussex Drive. June, 1952.

In 1868, the house of Gothic style was completed and the couple married. From the beginning, their new home took its place as one of the most exciting social centres in Ottawa. At the opening of "Gorffwysfa" in 1868, the Curriers held a reception for about 500 guests, including Sir John and Lady Macdonald. The house was filled with music and friends who had come to celebrate the couple's newly found happiness together.

Two years later, on February 16, 1870, the Curriers gave a ball at their home in honour of Prince Arthur of Connaught, later the Duke of Connaught and Governor General of Canada during World War I. As recorded in *The Canadian Illustrated News* the following week,

Lady Young's reception on the 15th (of February) was followed by the ball given by Mrs. Currier and our worthy and much respected Member of the 16th, in honour of the Prince. Mr. Currier's establishment is not on a very extensive scale, but all that was possible was done to render the occasion worthy of the hosts and of their distinguished guest. It was a source of much regret to Mr. and Mrs. Currier that necessity compelled a limitation of the invitation list, not at all in accordance with their generous inclinations. But with all, Ottawa has never before, at the hands of a private individual, presented an entertainment excelling this in elegance, and comfort and enjoyment ... A temporary ball-room was erected, which was fitted up and ornamented with a chaste and beautiful simplicity, though not without all the elaboration that good taste could supply . . . The ball-room was bright with gay and varied uniforms, and the tout ensemble presented as pretty and charming a picture as it is often possible to behold . . .

The generous host and hostess were unceasing in their exertions to promote the comfort and enjoyment of their company; and . . . feel assured, that the wines and refreshments were of the choicest and most costly that good taste and liberality could provide.

As the years passed, Joseph Currier continued to play an important role in the politics and business of his city and country. In 1882, he made the decision to resign from active politics, and shortly thereafter, he was appointed Postmaster for Ottawa. Two years later, he and Hannah decided to travel to Bermuda for a much needed rest. On their return trip in April of 1884, they stopped to visit friends and family in New York where, without warning, Mr. Currier died at the age of 64. Hannah returned to "Gorffwysfa", where she lived for another 16 years until her own death on January 26, 1901.

James, Joseph Currier's only surviving son, inherited the famous property. At the time he was living with his family at 190 Wellington Street, across from Parliament Hill, at the very centre of Ottawa. His father's house, on the other hand, was considered to be far out in the country. Because of the distance and the expense of maintenance, James reluctantly offered the elegant mansion for sale. On September 10, 1902, Mr. Currier's "place of peace" was sold to Mr. William Cameron Edwards for what was then considered the princely sum of $30,000.

THE EDWARDS

For the next forty-one years, "Gorffwysfa" belonged to members of the Edwards family, and during that time it remained one of the great centres of social and cultural activity in Ottawa.

Like his predecessor at "Gorffwysfa", William Cameron Edwards was both a highly successful lumber manufacturer and a politician. Once described by the *Montreal Herald* as being ". . . the life and soul of Liberalism in the Ottawa Valley", he was elected Member of Parliament for the riding of Russell in 1891, and continued to serve there until his defeat in 1900. Three years later, he was appointed to the Senate by his long-time friend and colleague, the Right Honourable Sir Wilfrid Laurier.

Senator Edwards's wife, Catherine Margaret Wilson of Cumberland, Ontario, also came from an old and distinguished family with a longstanding reputation in the business and political life of the community. Her brother, Norman F. Wilson, had been Member of Parliament for the Russell riding for a number of years, and his wife, Cairine, was the first woman to be appointed to the Canadian Senate on February 14, 1930.

In 1868, W.C. Edwards and a forwarding merchant named James Wood had established W.C. Edwards and Company, which operated a large steam sawmill at Rockland, Ontario on the Ottawa River east of Ottawa.

An exterior view of the home at 24 Sussex
Drive as built by J.M. Currier in 1868.

One of the main features in the drawing room of the original house was the elaborate fireplace, which was removed during the reconstruction in 1950. Also note the antique chandeliers and light fixtures.

In 1893, all the properties east of the Rideau Falls, including a cloth factory, a flour mill, a sawmill and the old Maclaren Mills west of the falls, were bought by W.C. Edwards and Company. Shortly thereafter, these were turned into a wood manufacturing complex consisting of a sash and a door factory, a planing mill and a mill for shaping hardwood lumber. At that time, the W.C. Edwards and Company sawmills at Rockland and in Ottawa were considered to be among the most extensive and prosperous in the Dominion. However, in 1891 all the mills to the west of the falls burned to the ground and, because of the decline in the lumber business after the turn of the century, were replaced by a single small mill.

W.C. Edwards's personal holdings were also impressive. During his lifetime, these included the property along what was then Sussex Street as well as a large piece of the property at Harrington Lake, which is now the summer residence of the Prime Minister of Canada.

In 1916, for personal and professional reasons, W.C. Edwards transferred ownership of the house on Sussex Drive, including its property and its contents, to his wife, Catherine. Following his death on September 17, 1921, Catherine lived in the house until her own death less than a year later.

In her will, Catherine appointed three executors and trustees to carry out the distribution of her property. For the year following her death, her sister, Edith Wilson, who had lived with Catherine and her husband for a number of years, was given possession of the house. The following year, the property, then known as 80 Sussex Street, was deeded to her nephew, Gordon Cameron Edwards, the son of W.C. Edwards's older brother, John.

The house that Gordon Edwards took over was an empty mansion on the edge of a cliff because, according to his aunt's will, all personal effects – rugs, furniture and even linen – were left to her sister, Edith Wilson. When Gordon Edwards, his wife, Edna Stewart Meighen (cousin of Prime Minister Arthur Meighen), and their two children moved into "Gorffwysfa" in 1923, they brought with them elegant and valuable furnishings, along with one of the most extensive private collections of European impressionist and post-impressionist painters in North America.

Like his uncle, Gordon C. Edwards was a lumber baron as well as a great lover and supporter of the arts. He could have passed his life quietly, enjoying his wealth and family position, but public duty and responsibility were a family tradition. This, coupled with his personal interest in politics, led him to run for office. In 1926 he was elected Member of Parliament for the riding of Ottawa. Coincidentally, that seat was originally held by Joseph M. Currier, the man who had built the house on Sussex Street over fifty years before.

Since it was first built in 1868, 24 Sussex Drive has been called home by many important families, all involved in the economic and political life of Canada. It is fitting that it has now become the home of the highest elected official in Canada, although the transition from private to public home was not a smooth one.

Government Expropriation

In the summer of 1943, with half the world, including Canada, caught up in the destruction of World War II, a chain of events began which would end the Edwards's ownership of 24 Sussex Drive and transform the magnificent old mansion into a modern building, the official residence of Canada's Prime Minister. By 1943, all the property to the southwest of the French Embassy, except a small parcel of land on Green Island as far as Earnscliffe, the former home of Canada's first Prime Minister, was owned by the federal government.

In that year, Emmett P. Murphy, the Deputy Minister of Public Works, wrote to the Honourable Alphonse Fournier, Minister of Public Works, setting out his department's suggestion that "for control purposes – the acquisition of the Edwards's property would now appear desirable, *in order that the same might not become commercialized.*" He added that the city had assessed the value of the property and house at $92,000, but that "... it is understood that the owner will expect a considerably higher figure." The letter suggesting expropriation was dated June 11, 1943. The Notice of Expropriation was dated July 15th and back-dated vesting of the property to June 12th – the day the memo was received by the Minister. This decision, which was to affect a family's life so radically and later force Gordon C. Edwards to spend the last years of his life fighting eviction battles in court, was made for no apparent reason. Granted, there had been talk in some quarters of the need for a home for Canadian Prime Ministers, but when the matter was presented to Prime Minister Louis St. Laurent in 1950 – seven years after expropriation – he insisted that he and his family did not want the house.

The Deputy Minister's worry that the property might become commercialized was equally ridiculous. The Edwards had no intention of selling their house and properties, and even if they had, they were not about to condone a sale that would "commercialize" their former family home. Furthermore, at that time cities were able to control where commercial ventures were established by zoning certain areas as residential and others as commercial.

On the basis of all available evidence, there was no possible argument for the government acting as if there were an emergency. In fact, six years after the expropriation, the Minister of Public Works advised the press that "... when the matters of policy (with respect to the use to which 24 Sussex would be put by the government) have been decided, we will be pleased to give the Press through the medium of the Department, whatever information should be made available."

Prime Minister Louis St. Laurent with his grandchildren, reading the Saturday comics.

Whatever the reasons for the government's actions, Mr. Edwards objected both to the expropriation itself and to the price offered by the government for his home and property.

The Crown suggested $125,000 for the house and properties, while Mr. Edwards claimed $261,190. On May 3, 1946, after three years in court, the Exchequer Court of Canada (now called the Federal Court) awarded Mr. Edwards $140,000 plus costs of $7,319.95 as final settlement for his home. During these three years when the question of compensation was before the courts, Gordon C. Edwards remained at his home at 24 Sussex Drive. Very shortly before the final decision was rendered, Prime Minister Mackenzie King replied to a question in Parliament that,

the property is being acquired in pursuance of the government's policy of securing title to valuable properties on the banks of the Ottawa River in order particularly to prevent their acquisition for undesirable uses.

Asked when the government would put into effect its plans for the Edwards property, the Prime Minister answered, "at an appropriate time, depending on circumstances." He then added that, "in the meantime the property continues to be occupied by Mr. Edwards." Gordon Edwards did remain in the house on a monthly basis, surrounded by the beautiful works of art he had so lovingly collected, until his death later that same year, on November 2, 1946.

Gordon Edwards left to his son, Maxwell, and daughter, Edna, the priceless family heirlooms and art collection he had acquired during his lifetime. But the major problem of what to do with the property still remained, causing the house and property to be left empty and unattended.

Now that they had it, the government still couldn't decide what to do with the property at 24 Sussex Drive. When suggesting a reason for its expropriation in 1943, the Deputy Minister of Public Works had included a number of possible uses to which the property could be put. His list included, among other things, the need for a residence for the Prime Minister, a domicile for the permanent staff at Government House, an office for the British Air Liaison Committee, or an office or residence for a foreign legation or embassy. Others had suggested using the house as a mess for officers serving at National Defence Headquarters, as office space for a government department, or as additional space for the National Art Gallery. But none of these ideas was accepted by the Department of Public Works.

Almost a year after Mr. Edwards's death, the house stood abandoned. The *Ottawa Journal* wrote on August 30, 1947, that

Both the gate and coach-houses are occupied by private tenants, while the old large stone house stands empty and deserted. There has been little maintenance work done. Many windows are broken, and the grounds allowed to run wild in grass and weeds.

*The coach-house on the Edwards property at
24 Sussex Drive, which was demolished
during reconstruction in the 1950's.*

The place was sadly in need of repairs. In 1944, a prominent Ottawa architect, Mr. W.E. Noffke, had already suggested that the total cost of repairs and renovations would be close to $190,000. Yet in a letter to Prime Minister Mackenzie King, dated May 5, 1947, the Honourable Alphonse Fournier, Minister of Public Works, wrote

It is impossible to estimate the expenditure without knowing the general type of occupation contemplated, but it might be roughly placed at $30,000.

The Swiss, Czechoslovakian and Norwegian legations were offered the use of 24 Sussex Drive, but they each decided against renting the property as it was only available on a short-term lease. Nor were they anxious to take on the financial burden of increasingly costly and necessary repairs.

From 1946 to 1949, the house and property continued to be a source of friction between bureaucrats and elected officials, who now had to deal with controversies involving the furnishings of the house and municipal taxes.

There was some question as to who now owned the elegant crystal chandeliers in the dining room and the antique light fixtures on the main floor. The executors of the Edwards estate insisted that these unique pieces were not to be included as part of the house, and sought either to remove them, or to have an additional sum paid for them by the government. Today, the chandeliers still adorn the dining room of 24 Sussex Drive, but the antique light fixtures were sold by the Crown Asset Disposal Corporation and no record remains of who purchased them.

There was also haggling over municipal taxes which, according to the lease, were the responsibility of the Department of Public Works, which, nevertheless, refused to pay them. The executors, completely frustrated by the slowness of the government department, were forced once again to take the matter to court. Fortunately, the Deputy Minister decided not to risk any further adverse publicity, and the problem was quickly resolved.

The Australian Embassy at 24 Sussex Drive

In late 1947 – four-and-a-half years after expropriation and a year after Gordon C. Edwards's death – the government found a tenant for 24 Sussex Drive. The Australian embassy, needing temporary office quarters, rented both the large house at 24 Sussex Drive and the smaller building at 10 Sussex Drive, which is now the home of the Prime Minister's chauffeur. At the time they moved in, the High Commissioner, the Right Honourable F.M. Forde, wrote the Minister of Public Works saying,

the main residence is obviously urgently in need of repairs as the timber on the front has rotted and requires replacing and all woodwork on the outside requires painting. Some of the rooms also require painting inside.

During the two years that the Australian embassy used the buildings and property, little repair was done. Superficial repairs were carried out on the house, but the major changes were being left until a final decision could be reached as to its use.

It was not until 1950, the last year of the Australians' stay in the house, that a decision was finally taken about the future of 24 Sussex Drive. At last the house was formally designated to become the home of Canada's future Prime Ministers.

Renovations

In the fall of 1949, E.P. Murphy, the Deputy Minister of Public Works, had written the Treasury Board, arguing that 24 Sussex Drive should be extensively ". . . altered, improved and repaired immediately." On November 23 of that year, the Treasury Board replied, agreeing with the Deputy Minister's submission to act immediately ". . . due to the urgency of the provision of accommodation for the Prime Minister." Two days later, the Deputy Minister wrote the Clerk of the Privy Council that repairs and improvements to 24 Sussex Drive were "considered to be a matter of pressing emergency in which delay would be injurious to the public interest."

In the minutes of Cabinet approved by the Governor General on November 29, 1949, the acting chief architect at the Department of Public Works, Mr. Gustave Brault, estimated the cost of repairs to be $168,000. He then advised that his draughting office could not handle the work required in the renovations of 24 Sussex Drive. As a result, the government proceeded to hire the Toronto architectural firm of Allward and Gouinlock to do the work. As work progressed, Mr. Brault revised his original estimate to $410,000.

The house at 24 Sussex Drive under reconstruction inside and out for use by Canada's Prime Minister.

The following is a breakdown of the original cost of providing a home for the Prime Minister of Canada.

1. Total of the main house including the architects' and contractors' fees	$278,550.91
2. Coach house	5,800.00
3. Gate house (later demolished)	2,900.00
	287,250.91
4. Furnishings	
a) furniture, drapes, rugs, decorations, etc.	80,000.00
b) silver, crystal, china, linen	20,000.00
c) stoves, refrigerators, deep freezers	5,000.00
	$105,000.00
5. Contingency item	17,749.00
6. Cost of land,	140,000.00
including Mr. G.C. Edwards's court cost	7,319.95
	$165,068.95
Total:	$557,319.86

The Prime Minister of the day, the Right Honourable Louis St. Laurent, was still not aware that the bureaucrats had selected a home for him in Ottawa. Mr. St. Laurent had never wanted an official residence for his family. His wife, Jeanne, preferred to remain in their Quebec City home, close to family and friends; and the Prime Minister was quite happy to spend his time in Ottawa at the Roxborough Apartments, where many of the Members of Parliament from all parties lived. When the decision concerning 24 Sussex Drive was presented to him as a *fait accompli* he accepted – but only on the condition that he pay rent as he had at the Roxborough, a practice which was to continue until 1971.

*English schoolgirls visit with Prime Minster
Louis St. Laurent at 24 Sussex Drive.*

From Elegant Mansion . . .

In trying to get an idea of the kinds and number of changes that had been made to the house at 24 Sussex Drive, I decided to speak to one of the members of the Edwards family, who could give me an impression of what it used to be like. Mrs. Mary Edwards, Gordon Maxwell Edwards's widow, kindly agreed to see me.

When I met Mrs. Edwards at her Ottawa home, I liked her immediately. Small and fragile in appearance, she thought that there was little she could offer me in terms of my research. But after this quiet and unassuming introduction, she began to recount some of her memories.

Late in his life, Mrs. Edwards's father-in-law, Gordon C. Edwards, proposed to sell his wonderful art collection to the National Art Gallery. This offer was turned down by the government of the day, citing lack of money as the reason for refusing this rare opportunity. It was not until 1972 that the tax act was changed, allowing Canadians to give works of art to the government in lieu of taxes.

Mrs. Edwards spoke of the time after her father-in-law's death in 1946, when she and a friend cleaned the house of all its furniture. It was the last opportunity she would have to hold and enjoy some of the exquisite articles before they were crated up and removed completely from the house.

"It was not so long ago," she reminisced, "that it was truly a beautiful place. They have changed it so completely."

She spoke of many of the changes that had occurred to the house after 1950. She showed me the Scottish wool carpet in warm crimson that was once part of the original carpet adorning the ten-foot-wide, oak-paneled stairs to the third floor at 24 Sussex Drive before the Department of Public Works removed the stairs completely during renovations.

She lamented the loss of the morning room. This room was considered a fine example of Adam design, with its clear, clean lines and the elaborate moulding around the fireplace. It is now a combination maid's sitting room and second kitchen.

She spoke of teas, dinners and parties, and many gatherings of family and friends. Marvellous parties and balls had been a part of the social life of her powerful, wealthy family. Her children, all grown now, had played in every corner of the stately mansion. There had been a billiard room in the basement where the men often gathered to test their skill and precision.

"It is hard for me to visualize how things must have looked then," I murmured, almost day-dreaming. "All the fireplaces, and paintings and woodworkings - it must have been wonderful."

"Yes", she replied quietly. "Would you like to see the pictures?"

*The main entrance at 24 Sussex Drive
during the time of the Curriers and
Edwards. The room through the centre door
served as the dining room.*

The dining room in the original house at 24
Sussex Drive, now the formal den. Note the
bay window and wood paneling, which were
removed during the reconstruction in 1950.

I could hardly believe my good fortune as Mrs. Edwards spread out before me all the pictures of that period that you see in this book, explaining to me the details of each room, the décor, the way it was changed after 1950, and her opinion of the changes.

Recounting her memories was nostalgic for Mrs. Edwards – fascinating and painful for me. Her memories were of a time long past, while mine, on that summer day, were very near.

. . . To Modern Residence

The pictures Mrs. Mary Edwards gave me marked the end of an era in the life of the home now known as 24 Sussex Drive. The process of expropriation, begun in 1943, was the beginning of a stage which would see the house completely gutted, remodeled and redecorated, before being reincarnated in 1950 as the official residence of Canada's Prime Minister.

The pictures in this book give the reader an idea of how dramatic the transition was from private home to public residence. Anyone who has seen the residence only as it is now would find it difficult to imagine what had been there before. Given the stately beauty of the original house, one might wonder why such a dramatic change was necessary. I can only hazard a guess as to some of the possible reasons.

First, it had been seven years since the property had been expropriated. Mr. Edwards knew that the court would decide against him. Indeed, the issue was not whether the house would be expropriated, but how much the government would be required to pay for the property. Following his death in 1946, the presence of a tenant on a short-term lease and the indecision about the final use to which the house would be put had delayed any major repairs or alterations of the house and grounds. It was still structurally sound, however, so the decision to rebuild the house, both inside and out, cannot have been necessary to remedy irreparable damage. In fact, W.E. Noffke, who had appraised the cost of repairs in 1944, wrote in his report presented as testimony before the Exchequer Court in the Edwards expropriation case that, since the building was in such a good state of preservation, the only items for repair or depreciation to be taken into account were the interior decoration, the exterior painting, new roofings, certain pipes and a justifiable depreciation in the value of the plumbing and heating pipes.

A view from the river of the Prime Minister's residence in April, 1951.

Second, 1950 was the time when everything modern was in vogue. What we now preserve religiously as heritage homes were then considered old monstrosities. The best thing an architect could prescribe for old buildings was demolition or complete remodeling, even if this meant replacing carved wooden panels with flat, white dry-wall, or changing antique light fixtures to modern ones, "straightening" bay windows, or building a wall where a window had been before. This was the age of bungalows in the suburbs; old houses near the heart of any city stood a great chance of being demolished and replaced by something new.

Finally, what was once "Gorffwysfa" was now to be the official residence of the Prime Minister of Canada. This house had to be on a grand scale, reflecting the position of the highest elected official in the land. Not only did the house have to be decorative, but it had to be functional as well. The Prime Minister has a private life as well as a public office, and he and his family would need rooms for their personal use. First and foremost, the house had to be an appropriate setting for a person who would also be a national symbol. In the end, the house was recreated to reflect this new role.

Major Changes After 1950

In the years following the 1950 renovation by the Department of Public Works, there would be only four major alterations to the house. In the 1960's the Pearsons enclosed and winterized the back patio into a spacious living area with a view of the Gatineau Hills. Later, in 1973, the Trudeaus modernized the main kitchen to resemble that of a large restaurant. The following year, they also altered the structure of the room on the second floor across the hall from the master bedroom from its traditional Victorian look, with its huge fireplace and bay windows, into what was then considered a modern room. This was popularly known as the "freedom room". Finally, in 1975, they added an enclosed swimming pool, sauna and sitting area to the west of the main house, and joined to it by an underground tunnel.

It is understandable, indeed inevitable, that each new family living at 24 Sussex Drive would have personal preferences for decorating the house. But it should be kept in mind that 24 Sussex Drive is a residence owned and maintained by the Canadian government. More important, it has been designated as a heritage home. As such, it is to be hoped that in the future, no alterations to the structure of the house will be made unless it has been determined that to do so will both enhance and preserve the essential history and character of the house.

The house at 24 Sussex Drive in April, 1951, ready for Canada's Prime Minister, the Right Honourable Louis St. Laurent.

Prime Minister and Mrs. St. Laurent with their Royal Highnesses Princess Elizabeth and the Duke of Edinburgh in front of 24 Sussex Drive. October 10, 1951.

Prime Minister and Mrs. Diefenbaker beside the lovely tulip beds at 24 Sussex Drive.

A Tour of 24 Sussex Drive

With the exception of those four structural changes, the house you would visit today is essentially the same one you have seen during the St. Laurents' stay from 1951 until 1957. Of course, new residents made changes, depending on their own personal tastes. Mrs. Pearson, for instance, created the Canadiana Room in the basement to commemorate our centennial year in 1967, and there have been many changes in décor over the past thirty years. But one of the realities of any official residence is that much of it remains the same. Certain pieces of furniture – pianos, lamps, tables, chairs, dishes and silver – always survive the change of residents, and 24 Sussex Drive is no exception.

In the spring of 1979, when my husband was elected Prime Minister, Cecilia Humphreys of Ottawa and her sister Maureen F. Lonergan of Winnipeg, both architects and personal friends, took on the special task of co-ordinating and overseeing the redecoration of 24 Sussex Drive. We chose as our main theme the history of Canada, and the changes we brought about are, on the whole, still evident today.

THE EXTERIOR

A high, wrought-iron fence runs along Sussex Drive. Further privacy is afforded by the pine trees which line the fence, screening the spacious grounds. A wide, semi-circular driveway makes a sweeping arch in and out of the grounds. The gatehouse which stood near the edge of the property was demolished in the 1950's to make way for this driveway. The former coach house, now known as 10 Sussex Drive, was remodeled in the 1950's to serve as a three-car garage, with rooms for the Prime Minister's chauffeur above it.

The house itself is built of local stone quarried in the Rockcliffe area, trimmed with limestone. Above the Georgian door, carved in stone, is the bottom quarter of the Canadian Coat of Arms, featuring three maple leaves on one stem.

*Guests share a joke during a lawn party
given in honour of the visit by President and
Mrs. Eisenhower to Ottawa in July, 1959.*

Prime Minister and Mrs. Diefenbaker pose with President and Mrs. Kennedy upon their arrival for a lunch at 24 Sussex Drive. May 17, 1961.

THE FIRST FLOOR

The main door at 24 Sussex Drive leads into a small foyer with a cloakroom and bathroom on the right. Proceeding up two steps, you arrive at the entrance hallway where guests are greeted and encouraged to sign a guest book. When the Diefenbakers lived in the house, two almost life-size oil portraits of them were hung on either side of the door. Mrs. Pearson added a deep strawberry-red Oriental rug and two antique portraits of Sir Alexander Croke and his wife.

After their marriage, the Trudeaus transferred two pieces of pine furniture to this hall – an armoire and a dresser – that had earlier formed part of Mrs. Pearson's Canadiana Room downstairs, and two other pieces were loaned to the residence by the Museum of Man to complete the furnishing of the main foyer. During our stay, we added two large paintings to the main foyer; one, by Jacques deTonnencour, was loaned to us by the National Art Gallery, and the other, by Henri Masson, was originally from the Firestone Collection in Ottawa.

Turning to the left of this main foyer, we pass a second powder room and enter the formal library, used mainly to receive guests and to give staff and other aides room to place phone calls during important meetings at the house.

I can remember coming home from the Bar Admission Course on the day in 1979 when the Alberta Premier and energy ministers had come to meet their federal counterparts to finalize the last details of an energy agreement. No less than 10 aides were crammed into this room, all trying to carry out their bosses' requests in confidence. Since they were all obviously nervous and frustrated at the lack of privacy, I decided to help the cause of federal-provincial relations by leaving the federal public servants where they were; sending the Alberta contingent to the family room of the second floor, and sending my husband's staff to his private office on the second floor.

In the formal library, shelves of books line one wall and both sides of the fireplace from ceiling to floor in this pine-paneled room. Mr. St. Laurent and Mr. Diefenbaker kept their law books here; my husband kept his books on Canadian art and history. Following our original theme of Canadian history, we hung Eskimo prints and carvings, displayed mounted dinosaur bones from the Badlands of Alberta, and kept archaeological and historical books on Canada's pre-history in this room. Our intention was to emphasize to Canadian and foreign visitors alike, the way of life and cultural contribution of our native peoples to the development of our nation.

As we proceed out of this room and to the right, we pass through a passageway between the library and the formal dining room. Here the Diefenbakers displayed a marble replica of the Taj Mahal and a carved teakwood palace from the King of Nepal. We added a table and mirror that had been gifts to the Canadian people from the Argentinian Ambassador during Mr. Trudeau's first term as Prime Minister.

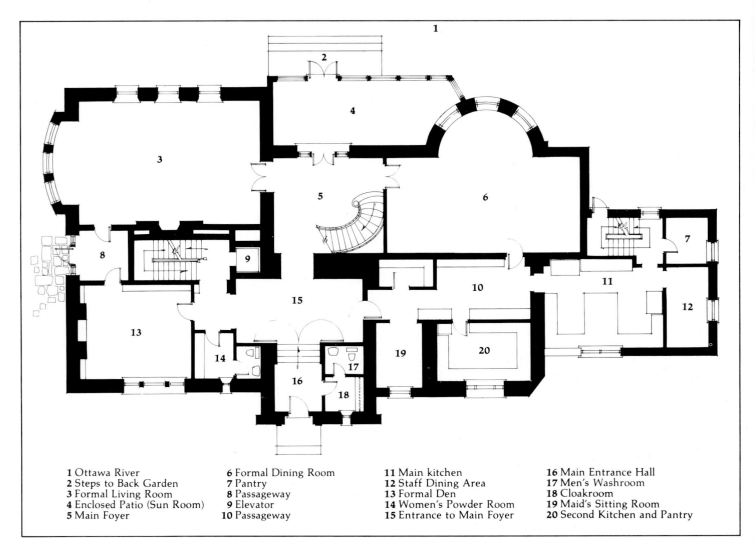

1 Ottawa River
2 Steps to Back Garden
3 Formal Living Room
4 Enclosed Patio (Sun Room)
5 Main Foyer

6 Formal Dining Room
7 Pantry
8 Passageway
9 Elevator
10 Passageway

11 Main kitchen
12 Staff Dining Area
13 Formal Den
14 Women's Powder Room
15 Entrance to Main Foyer

16 Main Entrance Hall
17 Men's Washroom
18 Cloakroom
19 Maid's Sitting Room
20 Second Kitchen and Pantry

Continuing through this passageway, we arrive in the formal living room. Depending on the weather, this room can be either warm and inviting or cold and austere. With windows looking out on both the west and the north, the room always presents interior decorators with the challenge of making the room look hospitable. A special committee of interior decorators from the three major Canadian department stores – Eaton's, Simpson's and Morgan's – had been chosen to redecorate 24 Sussex Drive after the 1950 renovations. They chose soft grey as the basic colour scheme, installing thick grey broadloom in the living room, the main lower hall, and the dining room. Muted-grey drapes of brocaded satin, two chintz sofas set by the fireplace, a settee in pink silk and a number of Empire armchairs with deep red velvet seats completed the living room arrangement for both the St. Laurents and the Diefenbakers.

Plan of the first floor at 24 Sussex Drive.

The main entrance at 24 Sussex Drive.
Note the old Canadiana furniture, part of
the donation to the residence by Canada
Steamship Lines to celebrate the Canadian
centennial. The large painting on the left is
by Henri Masson and those on the right are
by A.J. Casson. On the table is a wood
sculpture by Fred Moulding.

Formerly the dining room, with a bay window, side windows and paneling, this room off the main foyer is now the formal den, used for meetings with visiting heads of state.

*Mrs. Diefenbaker takes time out of her busy
schedule to petit point a chair cover in the
living room at 24 Sussex Drive.*

The grand piano provides one focal point for the living room, and has been placed either in the northeast corner by the doors leading to the lower main hall or in the bay window in the west end of the room, where it was during our stay. On a bright day, there is nothing more pleasant than to play the piano in the afternoon sun. In the evening, a pianist can be seen and heard by dinner guests in the formal dining room across the hall.

In the corner nearest the doors, where the piano had stood before our arrival, we placed an écritoire that had been a gift to the residence from Mrs. Walter Gordon in memory of her sister, Jane, late wife of the Honourable Bud Drury. On it we placed the original British North America Act, written in Sir John A. Macdonald's own hand while in London for meetings at Westminster in 1867, on loan to us by the Public Archives.

Although Mrs. Pearson left the walls and rug grey, she changed the colour of the furniture to suit her preference for subdued tones. A long sofa covered in Wedgwood blue material sat in the western alcove. The sofas were re-covered with a material that picked up the same blue, with a mixture of pale lemon yellow and olive green in its pattern. Two other chairs were redone in striped blue and green silk and two small blue, marbled-topped tables were set near the fireplace. The two antique, gold-framed Italian mirrors which hung on either side of the fireplace in Mrs. Pearson's formal living room were later placed in a storage room at Government House. In 1980, Mrs. Schreyer graciously arranged to have them repaired and sent over to us at Stornoway, where they now hang on either side of the main door.

Continuing past the double doors at the end of the living room, we come to the lower main hall. In the 1970's, the original grey broadloom in this hall was changed to beige wool rugs. When we were redecorating in 1979, we decided to remove the badly stained rug from the main hall, and replace it with a black and white tile floor to give us the only area where friends and guests could dance following dinner parties.

In this hall we find one of the very impressive structural features in this house: the spiral staircase, which winds its way gracefully to the second floor. Mrs. Diefenbaker often remarked to friends and journalists how unfortunate it was that her only daughter, Carolyn, had married before her famous stepfather had become Prime Minister. It certainly does seem to be a staircase made for a bride's elegant pose.

Guests at a small dinner party given by Prime Minister Clark and Ms. McTeer retire to the formal living room for coffee and liqueurs. 1979.

Prime Minister Clark helps his daughter Catherine put on her new cowboy boots.

In the main foyer, a stained and worn beige rug was replaced in 1979 to allow for a dance area. The watercolour and two prints (centre) are by Toni Onley, and the series of paintings on the stairway are by Michael Snow.

The bannister alongside the magnificent spiral staircase provides a great temptation for young children. One morning we caught our two-and-a-half year-old daughter, Catherine, halfway down the bannister, hanging on for dear life. Only the fright it gave her kept her from trying it again. I do not know if the Trudeaus were as successful with their boys.

But this staircase provides more than a temptation for adventurous children. It also provides a decorator with the main point of reference for the room. Mrs. Pearson hung a painting by Paul-Emile Borduas on the wall half-way up the stairs, its pale greens matching the Russian china statuettes of horses and sleighs on a table below. A painting by the late William Kurelek, depicting a log jam, reproduced the scene that takes place on the river below the back lawns.

Three of Michael Snow's "Walking Women" marched up the wall of the spiral staircase during our stay there. At a tea given for the Parliamentary Wives, we placed pots of tulips from the Governor General's greenhouse on every other step to make it look like an indoor spring garden, with splashes of pink and white against the beige rug. One water colour and two prints by the British Columbian artist, Toni Onley, were hung where Mrs. Pearson's Kurelek had been in the mid-sixties.

Through the French doors opening toward the north, we arrive at a glassed-in room that was formerly an open-air patio leading out to the back lawns. This room was closed in during the Pearsons' stay, and now offers a quiet haven of informality amid an otherwise formal first floor. Except on the very coldest days in winter, this room serves as a breakfast room and den for morning meetings, or as a reading room after dinner. Mrs. Trudeau decorated the space with patio furniture identical to the set in the pool area. Durable wall-to-wall broadloom carpet in light green made the area an ideal space for children to play on rainy days.

The moment I saw this large, empty space, I knew exactly what I wanted to do with it. In the summer of 1977, we had spent some time with friends in a converted farmhouse near Cape Cod. One of the rooms was decorated with comfortable, white wicker furniture, elegantly covered in Laura Ashley cottons. We chose similar material in a colourful blue and white pattern, which allowed us to treat this room as part of the first floor when entertaining. Throughout the summer months, guests always chose this informal, yet very attractive room to enjoy a quiet drink, rather than the more formal living room. It was here, at a desk of white wicker, that I answered many letters that year beneath one of Ottawa artist Alex Wyse's more elaborate and humorous sculptures, entitled "Exercising Flying Cows over the Governor General's Grounds", generously loaned to us from the Canada Council Art Bank.

Leaving this sun room, we now pass back through the hall with the spiral staircase and turn left into the formal dining room. Truly the most beautiful room in the house, the dining room has two outstanding features: the elaborately moulded ceiling and the bay windows overlooking the Ottawa River.

The original group of interior decorators in 1950 had had the walls painted a dark red to complement the grey rug. The ornate ceiling was entirely white, as was the moulded woodwork throughout. A long mahogany table, which seats

A caucus reception given by Prime Minister Clark and Ms. McTeer in the formal dining room to celebrate the 1979 election victory.

A formal dinner given by Prime Minister and Mrs. Trudeau for King Hussein of Jordan.

twenty-four, a smaller table by the bay window which seats eight, and two mahogany buffets at either end of the room used for serving at formal dinners, complete the furnishings of this magnificent room. The two chandeliers, installed in 1868 by the Curriers, still adorn the ceiling, and when lighted, accentuate its beauty.

The colour of the walls has changed with each new Prime Minister. The red of the St. Laurent period changed to blue when the Diefenbakers moved in. Later, Mrs. Pearson papered the walls in a pattern of cream and gold, Mrs. Trudeau with a coral Fortuny print, and I with a beige and white pattern.

Although elegant, the room has windows only on the north and tends to be quite dark. We felt that a light wallcovering, accompanied by high-gloss white woodwork and large, colourful and light-toned paintings would help to brighten it. I also felt that the ceiling was the room's main structural and aesthetic feature. We wanted to accentuate its splendour, and after much deliberation and with the help of one of the painters, we succeeded.

The painters who originally painted Stornoway for us, later performed the same task at 24 Sussex Drive. They were true craftsmen. Cecilia and her sister Maureen had suggested that spray painting the ceiling white would help accentuate its elaborate mouldings, yet even then, we were still not completely satisfied with the effect. It was certainly elegant, but the room still lacked something. Over dinner at the Lake the evening the ceiling had been painted, we discussed other rooms to be redone. But always, as if we had left something undone, the conversation returned to the dining room. It was the ceiling, we finally decided. Somehow it was just not right.

The next day we returned to the house and one of the painters, Mr. Roland Charron of Ottawa, with whom we had shared our thoughts, met us at the dining room door. He shyly escorted us into the alcove formed by the bay window.

"I have tried something special", he informed us quietly. "I hope it pleases you."

Looking up, we saw that he had painted parts of the elaborate design in gold leaf, highlighting the ceiling by emphasizing certain specific patterns in it. It was superb! And after we had all shaken hands and exchanged congratulations, we spent a happy day watching him change the ceiling into a work of art.

But the ceiling was not the only attraction of the magnificent dining room. When the table was set for a formal occasion with its place mats of Belgian lace and the state service in white and gold, the colour in the Wedgwood plates seemed almost a reflection of the gold in the ceiling, as it was filtered through the light of the two antique chandeliers. On one of the buffets, Sir John A. Macdonald's clock kept time, chiming each quarter hour. It was almost as if time stood still in this room, with its wonderful collection of exquisite pieces and blend of contemporary and traditional Canadian art.

No tour of a house would be complete without a look at the kitchen. Passing through the swinging door on the south wall of the dining room, we enter a passage which leads us to the large, restaurant-style kitchen, which is larger and better equipped than that found in most Canadian homes.

I learned quite soon after our arrival that in a house with a chef and servants, the kitchen becomes off-limits for members of the family. The pantry, the small dining area where the staff ate their meals, the staff sitting area – complete with colour T.V. – and the laundry room, were all areas where we were neither expected, nor welcome. This type of domestic arrangement was totally foreign to my background. In the farm country where I grew up, everyone congregated in the kitchen. It was the gathering place for family and friends alike – not only to eat, but to enjoy conversation and the smells of freshly baked food.

If I made one mistake about the house during our stay there, it was to allow myself to be excluded from the kitchen. Rare trips to the lake, where all my kitchen utensils had been sent, allowed me to relax, cook, bake and preserve to my heart's content. But during the time we spent in the main residence, I always felt like an intruder whenever I entered my own kitchen. Even Catherine would stand at the kitchen door and ask permission before entering the room.

On the east end of the second floor off the family room, there is also a small kitchen complete with a corningware top-stove and a compact refrigerator where one can make a late night snack. We would often make ourselves tea or hot chocolate there before bed to avoid the trek down the back stairs to the larger kitchen.

I can remember one night about a week after we had moved in when I had forgotten to stock the second floor refrigerator. I made my way downstairs in the dark around midnight to get some milk from the main kitchen. As I quietly closed the fridge door and turned to go back upstairs, I was startled by a man's voice asking what I was doing. Dropping both the mugs and the milk, I grabbed for a knife to defend myself, hoping frantically that my scream would be heard by the Mounties outside. It was also heard by my husband and the two live-in maids, all of whom came running to my rescue. To my great embarrassment, the man I was ready to attack was a security officer assigned, without my knowledge, to stay inside the house from midnight until 6 a.m. each day. Fortunately, he was not trigger-happy. My nerves were not quite so calm, and I must admit that it took something a bit stronger than milk to finally get me to sleep that night!

THE SECOND FLOOR

The second floor at 24 Sussex Drive has always been reserved for use as the private living quarters of the Prime Minister and his family. On the left at the top of the spiral staircase is the master bedroom. It is the same size as the formal living room beneath it, but its windows to the north provide an even better view of the river and hills beyond, and a small balcony to the west affords an excellent view of the Peace Tower in the distance. We chose a bedroom ensemble of dark mahogany. Over our bed hung a large-framed, quilted work, hand-painted on white silk, depicting a couple pronouncing their wedding vows. This sculpture, by Julia Schmitt-Healey of Halifax, was loaned to us by the Canada Council Art Bank, who provided both expert advice and excellent service in our search for other works by both new and established

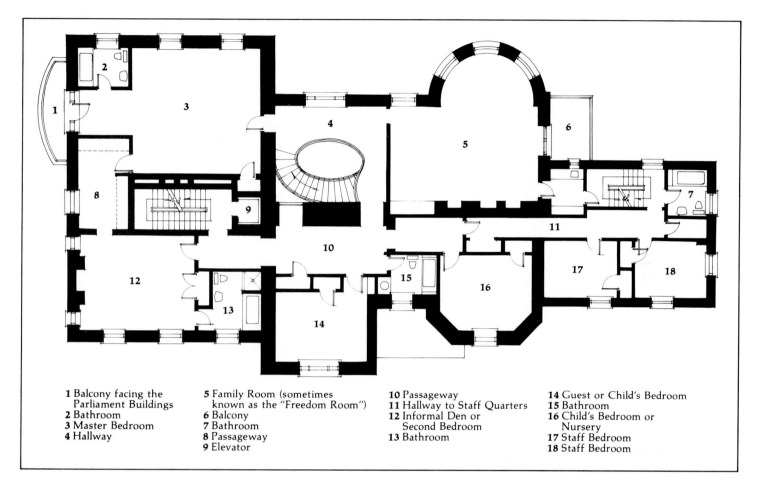

1 Balcony facing the
  Parliament Buildings
2 Bathroom
3 Master Bedroom
4 Hallway

5 Family Room (sometimes
  known as the "Freedom Room")
6 Balcony
7 Bathroom
8 Passageway
9 Elevator

10 Passageway
11 Hallway to Staff Quarters
12 Informal Den or
   Second Bedroom
13 Bathroom

14 Guest or Child's Bedroom
15 Bathroom
16 Child's Bedroom or
   Nursery
17 Staff Bedroom
18 Staff Bedroom

contemporary Canadian artists. When asked the title of this delightful sculpture one day, a friend jokingly replied, "Until the quilt doth us part, I suppose!", and it has been so called ever since.

The river behind the house that you can see through the bedroom windows is an incredibly active place. Each morning at about 6 a.m., from early spring until late autumn, rowers practice there. During the summer months, the blare of noise and music from nightly boat cruises passing by near midnight shock the sleeper awake. Small aircraft often take off from the water, and one fall day a hover craft was even being tested for its safety measures. Between boat tours and logging, the river behind 24 Sussex Drive is rarely quiet.

Across the hall from the master bedroom is what has become popularly known as Margaret Trudeau's "freedom room", modernized in an attempt to create a quiet corner where she could relax. Originally used by the St. Laurents as a room where family and friends could meet for an evening of cards, it

Plan of the second floor of 24 Sussex Drive.

served as a working sitting-room for both Mrs. Pearson and Mrs. Diefenbaker. The latter spent every morning there answering by hand as many as fifty letters.

We used this room as a place for relaxing quietly with family and friends, and to make it warm and inviting, we put in all our own furniture. As 1979 was the Year of the Child, we borrowed a series of pictures from an agency known as "All About Us". This agency encouraged and exhibited art work done by children from across Canada. The wall where we put up these pictures and the cupboard behind it became Catherine's corner, where she would play with her friends who came to visit.

The most arresting feature of this room is the spectacular view of the Ottawa River and the Gatineau Hills, and the little balcony on the far east end of the room provides an ideal place to sit quietly, study, read or simply daydream. Despite its airy spaciousness and lovely view, however, the room does lack privacy. A small kitchen leads to the staff stairs, and the door leading to the main hall on the far side of the room cannot be locked.

The windows which overlook the river and hills are built of one solid piece of glass, originally chosen, no doubt, to accentuate the spectacular view. But these single panes cannot be opened, with the result that the room is hot in the summer and cold in the winter. This meant that I had to have three space heaters installed below the windows to keep out the cold.

One of the funniest evenings I have ever experienced was the direct result of this heating problem. One evening after dinner, two close friends and I went upstairs to relax and listen to records. Within five minutes of turning on the space heaters and the lights, two fuses blew. We replaced them and, having turned off the space heaters, turned on the stereo. Two more fuses blew. Joking about not paying hydro bills, we replaced these fuses as well, then sat wrapped in mohair blankets, listening to the music from the excellent stereo by candlelight. Fortunately, our friends have a marvellous sense of humour.

After breakfast each morning, Mrs. Diefenbaker would answer as many as fifty letters in her upstairs sitting room. Today, the spouses of the Prime Minister and the Leader of the Opposition can draw upon the help of their social secretaries or executive assistants.

The upstairs sitting room was transformed in 1974 into what has been called Mrs. Trudeau's "freedom room". The Indian village scene on cork was a wedding gift from Mr. Trudeau's brother, Charles.

Prime Minister Trudeau plays with his son
Sasha on the front lawn of 24 Sussex Drive.

Mrs. Trudeau reads to her children in the
"freedom room". 1976.

There are three other rooms on the second floor, two of which serve as guest rooms, and a third with a fireplace, which is connected through a dressing room to the master bedroom. While it is now used as a working den for the Prime Minister, it was used previously as the personal bedroom for Mrs. St. Laurent, Mrs. Diefenbaker and Mrs. Pearson. Each decorated it to suit her own tastes. Mrs. Diefenbaker, for instance, painted the room mauve, and added brocaded curtains, bedspread and tufted headboard in the same shade to achieve a very feminine look. The pictures on her night and dressing tables and the walls were almost exclusively of her family.

The master bedroom on the other side of the dressing room used by Mr. Diefenbaker was painted dark green, and over the bed hung a portrait of his mother, as well as a colour picture of Sir Winston Churchill.

Because my husband and I did not use this second room facing Sussex Drive as a bedroom, we turned it into a den, where he could work and where I could study near the warmth of a huge fire.

THE THIRD FLOOR

An elevator on the right-hand side of the den connects the basement with the first and second floors, but to reach the third floor, you must climb a staircase. At the top of this staircase on the third floor is a small lobby where a telephone and bench are installed for use by guests. The rest of the attic is servants' quarters and bedrooms, added to the main house during the 1950 reconstruction, and separated by a thick door from the rest of the house. When Mrs. Trudeau redecorated the private section of the third floor in 1973, she redid these attic rooms with sloping ceilings in a most charming way to give the effect of four bedrooms in an old country inn.

THE REST OF THE HOUSE

Now that we have toured the first, second and third floors, only two parts of the house remain to be explored: the basement and the pool area.

When the Edwards lived at 24 Sussex, the recreation room in the basement served as a billiard room. Its wooden floors and paneled walls were made to specification in their own mills. During the 1950's reconstruction, the wood on the floor was changed, and the walls were redone in drywall and painted. This "rec" room was for the personal use of the Prime Minister and his family. The St. Laurents and the Diefenbakers hung coats there at large parties, while the small room beside it served mainly as a storage area for boxes and beverages.

But, in 1967, Mrs. Pearson made the room famous. When her husband was elected Prime Minister in 1963, plans were already underway for Canada's one hundredth birthday party, and in honour of our centennial, she created the "Canadiana Room". A long-time collector of Canadian art works and supporter of the arts in Canada, Mrs. Pearson began in 1964 to collect antique Canadian furniture from across the country. The pine board floors were covered by one large and several small hooked rugs from Montreal, taken from an old house in Ottawa. Most of the pine furniture was French-Canadian, from the old Tadoussac hotel in the province of Quebec. The pieces had been part of the

Once used as the private bedroom of the Prime Minister's spouse, this room is now a den, here decorated for use by Prime Minister Clark. Note the Chinese grass cloth installed by Mrs. Pearson, also used to decorate the dining room at Stornoway during the Peasons' stay there.

Mrs. Pearson smiles proudly at the press gathering for the official opening of the Canadiana Room at 24 Sussex Drive in November, 1966. The room, which required two years to furnish with early Canadian pieces from all over the country, was later dismantled by the Trudeaus to make a playroom for their children.

collection of William Coverdale, a former director of Canada Steamship Lines, which owned the Tadoussac hotel. At Mrs. Pearson's request, Mr. Roger McLaughlin, President of Canada Steamship Lines, generously offered the collection for use in her Canadiana Room.

On November 1, 1966, the room was opened to the press for a preview showing, and this description appeared in the *Ottawa Journal* the following day:

There's a subtle blending of old and new in the Canadiana Room, with its orange, grey and yellow homespun curtains and matching chair cushions . . . Over an antique pine mantle hangs one of the new Eskimo prints. On it is an Eskimo carving.

The collection of early Canadian pottery includes glazed plates, one of Sir Wilfrid Laurier and one of the Parliament Buildings. Mrs. Maurice Sauvé (now the Honourable Jeanne Sauvé, Speaker of the House of Commons), wife of the Forestry Minister, donated a colorful piece of pottery, which is displayed in a glassed-in pine cupboard. A small milking stool stands at one side of the fireplace, an antique cradle on the other. Two large "armoires" in the room have "mousetail" locks and hinges, indicating the late 1880's.

Several old books were arranged on a large table in the centre of the room. They include a book of rare cartoons from the library of Mrs. Pearson's father, old clippings from the Winnipeg Free Press, *the* Speaker's Book, *1898, when J.D. Edgar was Speaker of the House of Commons, and the first Hansard from the library of Sir John A. Macdonald.*

On the walls are prints of Indian tribes which were given to the Prime Minister when he was made a chief of the Blood Indian tribe in Alberta. There is also a color photograph of the inauguration of the new Canadian flag, February 15, 1965.

Pleased with her efforts and contribution to the preservation of our Canadian heritage, Mrs. Pearson is quoted as saying on that day, "Now it is collected. It took a long time, but it will be here I hope forever."

As is often the case, however, successors make changes, depending on their own tastes and needs. When 24 Sussex Drive was renovated and redecorated following the marriage of Prime Minister Trudeau, the Canadiana Room was dismantled and was later to serve as a playroom for his children. The furniture from the room was moved to other parts of the house and to Harrington Lake, where they remain today. The pieces, which include armoires, dressers, an antique cradle and table, are truly beautiful, and give to both residences an impression of the early traditions of this part of the country.

Through the door in the southwest corner of the recreation room is the passageway connecting the residence with the indoor pool, which was completed in 1970. The red cedar building was the gift of a number of unknown donors and is equipped with shower, bathroom, and sauna, and even a small kitchen. Attached to it is a glassed-in sitting area decorated with white patio furniture and filled with plants. It is a great luxury for a Prime Minister to be able to swim and enjoy a sauna each day in complete privacy, and in so doing, to keep fit and to forget for a few minutes the many cares attendant upon his position.

Whether a private home or a public residence, 24 Sussex Drive has always been at the centre of political life in Canada. It is a house of beauty and charm, providing a true "place of peace" for the people who have lived there.

These early pine chairs, chosen for the
Canadiana Room, are now at Harrington
Lake.

Her Majesty Queen Elizabeth and Prince Philip admire the gift from the Canadian people presented on their behalf by Prime Minister Lester B. Pearson during the Canadian centennial in 1967.

The pool, built in 1975, is enclosed by cedar walls. The pool area includes a sauna, shower, kitchen and sitting area, and is linked to the main house by an underground tunnel.

24 SUSSEX DRIVE
Home of Canada's Prime Minister

The formal den at 24 Sussex Drive during the stay of Prime Minister Clark and his family. It was used mainly to receive guests.

The formal dining room at 24 Sussex Drive after it was redecorated by Mrs. Trudeau in a cream and coral Fortuny print, with matching velvet used for the chair covers.

The formal dining room was redecorated in 1979 for Prime Minister Clark and his family. Parts of the ceiling were painted in gold leaf to highlight the elaborate design.

The formal living room during the stay of Prime Minister Clark and his family at 24 Sussex Drive.

The sun room, enclosed by the Pearsons during their stay at 24 Sussex Drive, was redecorated in 1979 for Prime Minister Clark and his family.

The family room on the second floor across from the master bedroom. Prime Minister Clark and his family used their own furniture in this room when it was redecorated in 1979. The windows, facing north, offer a spectacular view of the Ottawa River and the Gatineau Hills beyond.

HARRINGTON LAKE
Country Home of Canada's Prime Minister

An exterior view of Harrington Lake.
1979.

A view of the spacious living room at
Harrington Lake. It is identical in structure
to the dining room, with a fieldstone
fireplace filling the wall at the southwest
end of the house. A large window on both
sides of the fireplace offers a splendid view
of the lake.

STORNOWAY
Home of Canada's Leader of the Opposition

The main foyer at Stornoway following its redecoration in 1976. Through the centre door is the formal living room.

The upper foyer at Stornoway, identical in structure to the foyer in the main hall. The painting over the fireplace is by Ted Harrison, and on the wall to the left is a collection of children's drawings commemorating 1979, the Year of the Child.

The formal dining room at Stornoway following its redecoration in 1980. The butternut table and chairs with matching sideboard give a stately look to the room, while the paintings by Riopelle, Toni Onley and Frank Palmer add a contemporary look.

The formal living room at Stornoway in 1982. The Oriental rug at the centre of the room provides the main focus for the décor.

The master bedroom at Stornoway in 1982. Over the bed hangs a large framed, quilted work, handpainted on white silk by Julia Schmitt-Healey of Halifax, on loan from the Canada Council Art Bank.

Ms. McTeer reading to her daughter Catherine in the kitchen at Stornoway.

STORNOWAY
Home of Canada's Leader of the Opposition

The Past

THE MAJORS

Stornoway, the present official residence of the Leader of the Opposition, was built by Asconi Joseph Major, who bought the property at 541 Acacia Avenue in 1913 for $12,000 from Charles H. Keefer, one of the original custodians and developers of Rockcliffe Village. In 1889, A.J. Major's father, Sylvini, who had lived in Orleans, Ontario near Ottawa, had founded a wholesale grocery firm in what is now the Byward Market area of Ottawa. After Mr. Major Senior's untimely death in 1903, his wife, the former Marie Corinne Lebel, took over the family business and, with the help of her son, Asconi, built it into one of the largest firms of its kind in eastern Canada. The company merged with a number of others in 1925 to form National Grocers Limited, and Mrs. Major, one of the leading businesswomen in Canada at the time, remained active in the business life of the community until her death in 1947.

In 1913, when Asconi Major bought the property in Rockcliffe Village, he was already a well-known businessman in Ottawa. He was married to the former Corinne Parent, whose father, the Honourable Simon-Napoléon Parent, had been Liberal Premier of Quebec from 1900 to 1905. By 1913, they had two children, Paul and Robert. They chose to build their home in the rural setting of Rockcliffe Village, but within commuting distance by horse and buggy to the family business in Lowertown near downtown Ottawa.

In 1915, a year after the construction of their now famous home was completed, a third son, Wilfrid, was born to them, named after his godfather, Sir Wilfrid Laurier, then Prime Minister of Canada.

In 1923, when the Majors decided to move downtown to be closer to their business and schools for their children, they did so reluctantly. They loved their mansion out in Rockcliffe Village and wanted their children to be raised in a country environment. But the horse and buggy was still the main mode of transportation in Ottawa in those days, and it was most inconvenient and tiring to be continually battling inclement weather in all seasons to travel into the city and back each day.

During the winter, a horse and sleigh, replacing the buggy, would be sent out to Rockcliffe from the Majors' York Street warehouse to pick up Mr. Major and the children, and to take them, bundled in Buffalo hides, into Ottawa. Soon it became obvious that the inconvenience was too great, and in April of 1923, the Majors sold their home to Mrs. Ethel Perley-Robertson for $40,000. Sir George Perley, Mrs. Perley-Robertson's father, had been a member of the Imperial Privy Council, and Member of Parliament for the riding of Argenteuil, Quebec, from 1904 to 1938.

Stornoway, around 1914, just completed for use by the Major family.

A wedding in the Major family,
around 1918.

The main living room at Stornoway, around 1917. Note the photograph of the Prime Minister of the day, Sir Wilfrid Laurier, godfather to the Majors' third son.

THE PERLEY-ROBERTSONS

Shortly after their arrival, the Perley-Robertsons baptised the home they were to live in for the next two decades "Stornoway", after Stornoway on the Isle of Lewis in the outer Hebrides that had been the ancestral home of the Perley family.

Mr. and Mrs. Perley-Robertson had been married in St. Margaret's, Westminster in 1917 and, when they moved into Stornoway in 1923, had three children – a daughter, Jean, and twin sons, Alexander and George. Two other daughters, Anne and Clair, were born after the move, but unlike the Majors' son, neither was born at home.

After they had moved into the house, the Perley-Robertsons commissioned the architect, Allan Keefer, who had originally designed the house, to carry out certain renovations. These included the addition of a bathroom and three bedrooms above the kitchen to accommodate staff as well as living quarters above what was once the stable and was now a three-car garage.

I had the good fortune to meet the late Mrs. Perley-Robertson at a tea in Rockcliffe once, where she enthusiastically answered all my questions about the house and even sent me a long letter full of historical and family details. When our daughter Catherine was born the following year, Mrs. Perley-Robertson sent me a rose with a note saying, "To celebrate the birth of another daughter born at Stornoway."

THE DUTCH ROYAL FAMILY AT STORNOWAY

While Stornoway has housed six Leaders of the Opposition and their families since 1948, it is most famous as one of the two houses in which Princess Juliana of the Netherlands stayed during her sojourn in Canada during World War II.

Following the invasion of the Netherlands by the German Army on May 10, 1940, Princess Juliana, her husband and two daughters escaped in an armoured truck from the Hague to Ijmuiden on the North Sea, where H.M.S. *Codrington*, took them to safety in England. After a short stay in that country, it was decided that she must leave for Canada with her children. They boarded the Dutch ship *Sumatra* docked in Cardiff, Wales, for the transatlantic crossing to Halifax.

Upon their arrival in Ottawa in the early summer of 1940, Princess Juliana, her daughters and entourage lived for some four months at Government House with the Governor General of the day, the Earl of Athlone and his wife, Princess Alice, who was Princess Juliana's aunt and godmother to her eldest child, Princess Beatrix.

In the fall of 1940, they moved to 120 Lansdowne Road in Rockcliffe Park, overlooking MacKay Lake, which had been the residence of the late Shirley E. Woods. Princess Juliana's husband visited them in the summers of 1941 and 1942, and during this second visit the family moved to Stornoway.

The Perley-Robertson and Wallace families
at Stornoway in the early 1920's.

Ottawa in 1942 was the centre of a nation at war. Experts from across the country were travelling to Ottawa to help with defence and other matters relating to Canada's war effort abroad. Available accommodation was at a premium. One effect of the influx was to increase rumours that people with large houses and empty bedrooms were to be asked to take in boarders. Knowing that Princess Juliana found the house at 120 Lansdowne Road too small for her family, Mrs. Perley-Robertson offered her home to the Dutch royal family, and Princess Juliana accepted her gracious offer.

The house was to be rented furnished, as the royal family had been able to bring only one suitcase each when they had fled Holland. Furthermore, they had no desire to spend precious funds – funds that were needed for their country's war effort – on furnishing a rented house.

Mrs. Martine Feaver, who still lives in Rockcliffe Village today, was one of Princess Juliana's closest friends. She and her daughter had escaped with the Dutch royal family at the beginning of the war and lived with them during their stay in Ottawa, as did another personal friend, Miss Feith, who acted as nurse to the young princesses.

The daily routine of the Dutch royal family during their stay at Stornoway was peppered with visits from foreign dignitaries, including Madame Chiang Kai-shek. During her stay in Canada, Princess Juliana worked hard for the Dutch cause, meeting Dutch warships, visiting Dutch families, and paying official visits to other countries. Her children attended Rockcliffe Public School nearby and could be seen bicycling each day around the village with their friends.

On January 19, 1943, Princess Juliana's third child, Princess Margriet was born at the Ottawa Civic Hospital. To ensure that no future problems would arise with respect to her nationality, the Canadian Parliament passed a special law declaring extraterritorial the suite of rooms where the young princess was born. The princess was delivered by Dr. John Puddicombe, a well-known and respected Ottawa doctor. Thirty-three years later, his son, Dr. Paul Puddicombe, delivered our daughter Catherine while we were living at Stornoway.

Queen Wilhelmina came from London, where she lived in exile during the War, to attend her granddaughter's christening in Ottawa. The godfathers were the Governor General, the Earl of Athlone, and U.S. President Franklin D. Roosevelt; while her godmothers were Queen Mary of England and Martine Roell (now Feaver).

The Dutch princesses with Princess Juliana in the garden at Stornoway.

The Dutch royal family, including Queen
Wilhelmina, pose for a formal portrait
outside Stornoway, following the christening
of Princess Margriet.

Preparations for a press session on the front lawn of Stornoway before the Dutch royal family return to Holland in the summer of 1945.

From Private Home . . .

Mr. Robert Major, a Member of Parliament from Quebec from 1968 to 1972, and a prominent member of the insurance community in Montreal, had moved to Ottawa with his wife in late 1970. I was anxious to hear his memories of my home when it was a private residence built by his father, and suggested that he come to Stornoway in the hope that seeing the place again would trigger memories of his life here. I can remember feeling awed as I gave Robert Major a tour of the house that spring day. His memories gave me a feeling of belonging to an historical whole. As we entered the master bedroom, for instance, he quietly remarked that this had been his mother's personal bedroom, and the room where his younger brother, Wilfrid, had been born.

By his words, he had made Stornoway seem more than an official residence where we happened to be staying. It was a place where families had lived, where children had been born and raised, where people had lived and died. It had been a home, and the presence of my family there was an indication that it still was. The house had given all who stayed there shelter and comfort and in return, we had added to its history.

. . . To a Home for the Leader of the Opposition

One of the first people to give serious consideration to the possibility of a publicly-funded residence for the Leader of the Opposition was Senator Grattan O'Leary. Although a "Party" man to the core, he had a love and respect for parliamentary democracy which transcended mere political partisanship.

One evening in 1946, Senator O'Leary had visited Mr. St. Laurent, then Minister of Justice and Canada's representative at the United Nations, at his home in the Roxborough Apartments. He left after that visit, thinking that living in an apartment was not suitable for any person required to fulfill the political and social obligations imposed on him by high public office.

"So I determined," Senator O'Leary said later, "that I would see what I could do to obtain a home for the Opposition Leader which would be consonant with the dignity of his position."

In an attempt to collect enough money to buy a suitable house in Ottawa, Senator O'Leary immediately began to visit friends and acquaintances in Ottawa, Montreal and Toronto. The first person whom he approached was Mr. J.W. McConnell, who had been his campaign manager during the 1925 election in Gaspé, Quebec. A gift of $10,000 and names of ten other donors encouraged Senator O'Leary to continue his efforts.

Mr. Stanley McLean, another acquaintance of Senator O'Leary, was so enthusiastic about the idea that he hosted a luncheon for a small group of wealthy friends, among them the late Senator Wallace McCutcheon. After Mr.

Catherine Clark says "Hello, Grandpa" to Mr. Diefenbaker at an annual lawn party for members of the P.C. caucus and the parliamentary press at Stornoway. June, 1978.

McLean explained the idea about a home for the Leader of the Opposition, those in attendance pledged $35,000 for the purchase.

When the Perley-Robertsons had moved back to Stornoway after the return of Princess Juliana and her family to the Netherlands, they found it too big for their needs. Upon hearing that a house was needed for the Leader of the Opposition, Mrs. Perley-Robertson offered to sell Stornoway for only $55,000, and on March 21, 1950, the Royal Trust Company purchased it.

Over the years, the Trust that had been set up to purchase and oversee the running of the house raised almost $200,000 from supporters of both political parties in Canada. In late 1969, on the advice of friends, Senator O'Leary, the sole surviving trustee, went to the newly-elected Prime Minister, Pierre Trudeau, to explain to him that the Trust could no longer afford to keep up the house. He had already spent, he explained, some $2,000 of his own money to pay municipal taxes on the property.

The house had not been redecorated since the Pearsons had lived there in 1958; and more than a decade later, it was in great need of major repairs. Furthermore, the acre of garden was overrun and required the attention of a full-time gardener, which was also beyond the Trust's means.

After discussing the matter with his officials, Mr. Trudeau agreed that the government would purchase the property, and on January 1, 1970 it did so, for the consideration of one dollar. Since then, the house and garage have been maintained by the Department of Public Works, and the grounds by a full-time gardener employed by the National Capital Commission.

The Exterior

The house that the architect, Allan Keefer, designed before the First World War was distinctive in two special ways. All the houses he designed in Rockcliffe Village during those years, which included the present Swedish embassy, Coltrin Lodge, and the present embassy residence of the United Arab Republic, had certain features which marked them as "Allan Keefer houses". Stornoway was no exception. It had the Keefer trademarks of a porte-cochère at the north end of the structure, and an openness of design which allowed one to enjoy an unobstructed view from one end of the house to the other.

In 1978, officials at the Department of Public Works decided that the porte-cochère was unsafe and a danger to persons walking under it. Not wanting it to be altered in any way, we had a number of friends – both architects and engineers – inspect it for safety. All declared it structurally sound. Weeks of arguing ensued until finally, the department officials, determined to tear it down, advised us that for insurance purposes we would be held personally liable for any injury that might occur due to the porte-cochère. Two weeks later, the demolition began, with bulldozers and heavy equipment finally destroying what was the most interesting structural aspect of the house. The inside walls were cracked by the endless hammerings and all those who had long known the house were shocked and disappointed by its appearance without the famous porte-cochère.

Private Maintenance

Until 1971, when the government formally took over Stornoway as one of its official residences, all repairs and maintenance had been paid for by donations from wealthy and concerned Canadians via the Trust.

Unlike 24 Sussex Drive, which had been carefully redecorated at public expense by a committee of decorators, the Stornoway that greeted the Drews in 1950 was empty of all furnishings.

Private means allowed George Drew, Leader of the Opposition from 1948 to 1956, to decorate and furnish the house in a grand and elegant style, overseen by his beautiful and highly artistic wife, Fiorenza. They kept their own servants, and people they entertained there still remember the priceless family heirlooms that Mrs. Drew had used to decorate her Ottawa home. The daughter of Edward Johnson, a long-time general manager of the Metropolitan Opera in New York, Mrs. Drew's influence was felt throughout the house. The drawing room for instance, was painted in pale turquoise, one of her favourite colours, with matching drapes from ceiling to floor. The furniture was upholstered in a bright chintz, and the whole atmosphere was one of formal elegance.

When Mr. Drew was appointed Canadian High Commissioner to London in 1957, his successor, the Right Honourable John G. Diefenbaker, refused to move into Stornoway, convinced that the election expected within a few months would result in his being elected Prime Minister. He was right.

Following that election in June of 1957, Mr. St. Laurent made the personal decision to remain only as interim leader of his Party. As he planned to return shortly to his home in Quebec City, he decided against moving into Stornoway. For the next year, the residence of the Leader of the Opposition stood empty.

Public Trust

Following the Diefenbaker sweep in 1958, the Pearsons prepared to move into Stornoway. But with the house in great need of repair, especially from water damage suffered during the year it had stood unoccupied, they were faced with the prospect of spending thousands of dollars to decorate, repair and furnish Stornoway before they could use it as their home. Aware that the house had to be redone, Senator O'Leary authorized Mrs. Pearson to do whatever was needed, asking merely that she send him the bills. She took him at his word, and proceeded to redo completely the stately, old Rockcliffe mansion.

*Mr. and Mrs. George Drew and family in
the garden at Stornoway. July 8, 1953.*

Lester B. Pearson and Mrs. Pearson
standing in front of Stornoway. October 22,
1958.

A Tour of Stornoway

Stornoway is a very different place from 24 Sussex Drive. It is much smaller, more manageable and better suited to family living. Situated in Rockcliffe Village, it is surrounded by other nearby homes, not isolated on a cliff, as is the house at 24 Sussex Drive. The grounds are larger and their layout lends itself more easily to outdoor entertaining than the Prime Minister's grounds.

After the house became a government residence in 1971, two major alterations were made by the Department of Public Works. First, a new electrical system was installed throughout the house. Then the entire house was repainted in what can only be described as institutional pink and green. Mary Stanfield, who was living at Stornoway at the time, was not consulted on the matter of the colour scheme. She was horrified to discover that the pink paint on the living room walls clashed with her peach satin-covered love seats and curtains. Always one to make the best of every situation, she used to joke that she was really setting a new style!

Aside from these two changes and the removal of the porte-cochère by the Department of Public Works, the house has remained basically the same as it was after the Pearsons had it redone in 1958. Just as with 24 Sussex Drive, however, Stornoway has often been partly redecorated with each new set of residents to suit their personal tastes and needs.

Mr. and Mrs. Diefenbaker with their dog,
Happy, in the garden at Stornoway.

The Honourable Robert L. Stanfield relaxes in the formal living room. 1972.

Mr. Stanfield clearing snow from the walks
at Stornoway. Until 1971, it was up to the
occupant of the day to keep the snow cleared
and the gardens weeded. Now these jobs are
handled by the National Capital
Commission.

THE FIRST FLOOR

The main door of Stornoway faces Acacia Avenue and leads into a large foyer featuring a fireplace with an ornate wooden mantle. Right inside the door is a high vaulted ceiling with an elaborately moulded relief, which is repeated in the hall to the north, off the main foyer leading to the side door. Today, two Italian gold leaf mirrors hang on either side of this main door. These mirrors are those which once hung on either side of Mrs. Pearson's fireplace at 24 Sussex Drive. When my husband and I returned to Stornoway in 1980, Mrs. Schreyer immediately answered my request to borrow these mirrors, and even arranged for them to be repaired before sending them over.

To the immediate right of the main entrance is the staircase leading to the second floor; and beside it is a room which has been used either as a library or family room or both since the house was built. Princess Juliana's secretary used it as his office to work on official and domestic business when the Dutch Royal family lived here during the war years. Mr. Drew entertained the Right Honourable Louis St. Laurent here when the latter, as Prime Minister, visited him for lunch after mass on the Sundays he remained in Ottawa. Indeed, Mr. St. Laurent had been quoted on many occasions as saying that he preferred the comfort of Stornoway to that of 24 Sussex Drive – no doubt because he had to spend so much time alone there.

To the left of the main foyer is the formal living room, with a fireplace whose elaborate wooden mantle is similar to the one in the main foyer. Because of its northeastern exposure and its size, the room receives little natural light each day.

When we moved to Stornoway in 1976, it was in great need of maintenance and redecoration. Like the Pearsons, we did not have enough personal furniture to fill the whole house, and chose to put our things on the second floor, which has always been used as private family quarters.

Cecilia Humphreys came to our rescue and put together some ideas for redoing the first floor. Budgetary considerations as well as the fact that I was pregnant and working on my legal studies at the time, forced us to leave the second and third floors until a later date.

When we started redecorating in March of 1976, we first turned our attention to the formal living room. Following Cecilia's proposal, the formal living room was to be one of the most inviting rooms of the house. At the centre of the room is an Oriental rug which Cecilia had found rolled up in the Governor General's storage rooms in 1976, and which has formed the starting point for all our decorating ideas ever since. In order to make the room warmer and more intimate, we painted the walls chocolate brown with all the woodwork, the fireplace mantle and moulding, a high-gloss white. It had taken some coaxing from Cecilia and her sister Maureen to convince me that it was the right choice. But once the work was completed, the effect was so dramatic that I was sorry I had ever doubted them. The contemporary art we chose with the help of Karen Love, formerly of the Canada Council Art Bank, gave a stunning and

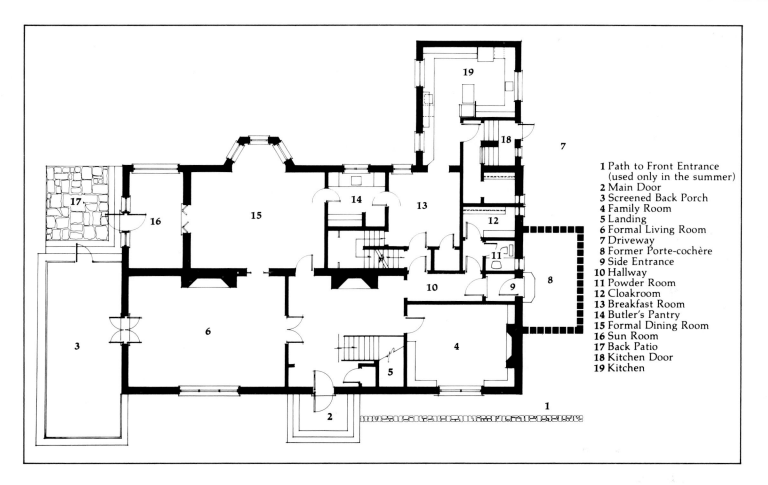

1 Path to Front Entrance
  (used only in the summer)
2 Main Door
3 Screened Back Porch
4 Family Room
5 Landing
6 Formal Living Room
7 Driveway
8 Former Porte-cochère
9 Side Entrance
10 Hallway
11 Powder Room
12 Cloakroom
13 Breakfast Room
14 Butler's Pantry
15 Formal Dining Room
16 Sun Room
17 Back Patio
18 Kitchen Door
19 Kitchen

Plan of the first floor of Stornway.

memorable effect to this important room. Since then, this room has been twice redone, once with a grey material, by Mr. Trudeau and later, the colour it is today – a Wedgwood blue, again contrasting the white high-gloss woodwork.

Passing through two solid sliding doors, we come to the main dining room. Its bay windows overlook the impeccably groomed garden to the west, and a lovely sun room to the south. In 1958, Mrs. Pearson had the walls above the dado covered in a golden Chinese grass cloth, which remained there until 1979, when it was removed, along with the dado, by Mr. Trudeau's decorator. The walls were then covered in a cream material with red dots, which was also used for matching curtains hanging in the bay window overlooking the western part of the garden. As he had already made plans to return to private life, no paintings or other art were hung or displayed during Mr. Trudeau's stay at Stornoway.

The family room off the main foyer during the stay of Mr. Joe Clark and his family.

Upon our return to Stornoway in April of 1980 the dado was replaced and painted white, as was all the woodwork and the louvred shutters in the bay windows and doors leading to the sun room. The butternut table and twelve chairs with matching sideboard have been in the house for years: the Victorian green walls, with paintings by Riopelle, Toni Onley and Frank Palmer, create a stately, yet contemporary look to this room.

The sun room on the south end of the dining room has windows on two sides and a charming cobbled floor. A window-box is filled with plants and colourful flowers all year round, and together with several hanging plants, brings the outside in for us to enjoy. This room has been used almost exclusively as a breakfast-sitting room where close friends can join us for quiet lunches or dinners during the summer months. We put Alex Wyse's famous work "Exercising Flying Cows over the Governor General's Grounds" in this room, as it is guaranteed to make the face of even the stiffest visitor break into a smile.

The large porch just outside and to the left of the sun room was screened in some forty years ago, and is used throughout the summer and fall for receptions and teas.

Connected to the dining room by a butler's pantry is the family breakfast room and the kitchen. The kitchen has always been terribly underequipped, which makes entertaining for large numbers most difficult. But here again, I have been saved on numerous occasions by generous and talented friends. While I was still at law school, three friends, Jean Pigott, Grete Hale and Gay Cook, joined forces to help ensure that every major social event at Stornoway was a success. Together we planned everything from strawberries and champagne on the lawn for almost a thousand press people to lunches and teas for various groups and organizations. Whenever I asked, they were ready and willing to use their experience to ensure that each and every event was well organized.

In the dining room, Mr. Clark serves wine
to guests invited to the annual Clark/
McTeer Christmas tree-cutting party.
December, 1980.

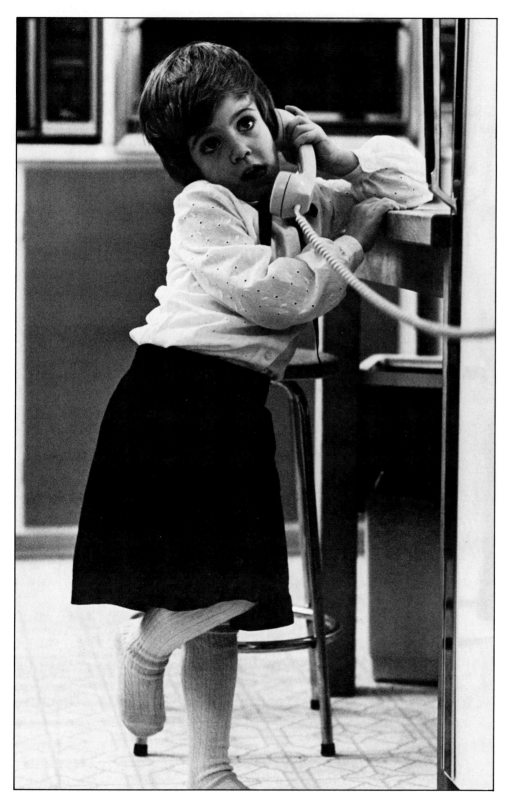

Catherine Clark chats on the telephone in the kitchen at Stornoway. February, 1982.

THE SECOND FLOOR

As mentioned earlier, the second floor is given over entirely to the family's private quarters. At the top of the stairs is a large foyer identical to the one of the main floor. Over the working fireplace hangs a painting of children playing by the Yukon artist, Ted Harrison, that complements the collage of children's drawings that fill the wall on its left.

Off this second floor foyer are two large rooms. To the right is a guest bedroom with complete bathroom, which was originally Mr. Major's bedroom, and most recently has been used as a guest room. The fireplace makes it particularly cosy on cold winter days. Friends who visit have been known to find it difficult to trade its warmth for their cross-country skis. The original porte-cochère was built off this room.

The second room has a southern exposure overlooking the garden, and is one of the brightest places on the second floor. Originally the bedroom of two of the Major's sons, it has since been used as Princess Beatrix's and Irene's room, Mimi Stanfield's bedroom, a guest room, and now it is my husband's private den.

A door from this room leads to the wing formerly referred to as the servants' quarters, which was built shortly after the Perley-Robertsons moved into Stornoway in 1923. It is now used as bedrooms and playrooms for children.

The master bedroom on the northeast corner is really a suite of rooms, including the bedroom itself, as well as a bathroom, a change room and a sun room, situated directly over the one downstairs. Mrs. Diefenbaker had numerous shelves built in the change room to store her many hats; the master bedroom is equipped with a cedar cupboard to store clothes properly between seasons. The sun room, which is now my den, is furnished in white wicker. Filled with my books and plants, this bright, airy little room overlooking the garden is my own private corner for reading and working.

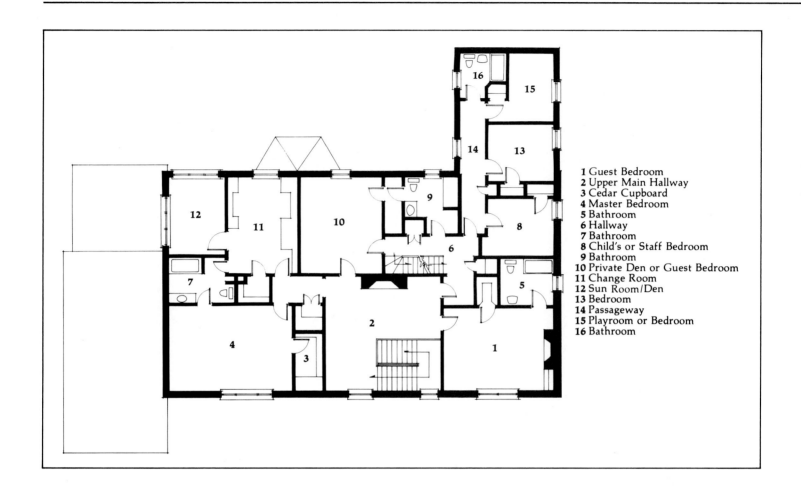

1 Guest Bedroom
2 Upper Main Hallway
3 Cedar Cupboard
4 Master Bedroom
5 Bathroom
6 Hallway
7 Bathroom
8 Child's or Staff Bedroom
9 Bathroom
10 Private Den or Guest Bedroom
11 Change Room
12 Sun Room/Den
13 Bedroom
14 Passageway
15 Playroom or Bedroom
16 Bathroom

Plan of the second floor of Stornoway.

The guest bedroom on the second floor
during the stay of Mr. Clark and his
family. The quilts were handmade by an
aunt of Ms. McTeer.

The private den of Mr. Clark, on the second floor of Stornoway.

*Catherine Clark's bedroom on the
second floor at Stornoway.*

Ms. McTeer in her den, on the second floor
of Stornoway. June, 1982.

THE THIRD FLOOR

The third floor of Stornoway is large and spacious, with a suite of two rooms and a bathroom designed for a nanny, and a large room that was once a billiard room and is now a playroom. Off it is a sewing room, where I try each year to make creative Christmas gifts. Anyone on my list will know that my creative impulse far exceeds my sewing ability.

Looking back at my stays at Stornoway and 24 Sussex Drive, I am aware of the many differences between the two residences. Personally, I found Stornoway more to my liking because its scale and situation were better suited to family life. I also found the garden more beautiful at Stornoway; and there were no bitterly cold winds blowing off the river, as there were at 24 Sussex Drive.

Stornoway has often been referred to as a transition house, where prominent public people live on their way into or out of active political life. The implication seems to be that Stornoway is a lesser house than 24 Sussex Drive. Yet I will always remember Stornoway fondly as having been a very important part of my family's public and private life.

HARRINGTON LAKE
Country Home of Canada's Prime Minister

The Past

Harrington Lake, nestled between Meach Lake and Lac Philippe, is situated in the province of Quebec, about twenty miles north of Ottawa. The lake itself is deep and almost four miles long, with high, rugged banks on all sides. Much of the forest around it was consumed by fire in 1915, so today only deciduous trees remain to exhibit their multicoloured leaves each autumn.

Like that of 24 Sussex Drive, the history of Harrington Lake is closely linked with that of the lumber industry. In fact, parcels of land around the lake were at one time owned by W.C. Edwards, who also owned 24 Sussex Drive.

But unlike this later owner, the original families who settled the land around the lake in the 1840's were poor Irish immigrants, fleeing famine and economic depression at home. The Grey Nuns took charge of these destitute people, providing them with small plots of land in and around this part of the Gatineau Hills, where most built log cabins and tried for a few years to eke a living out of the marginal soil. For a time in the late nineteenth century, this whole area was full of families with Irish names: Gillespie, Deans, Healey, Flynn, Farrell, Quinn and Fennerty. But by 1914, for economic as well as personal reasons, almost all of them had moved on to other places.

According to records maintained by the National Capital Commission, the Harringtons are listed as the first family to settle on the lake. They are said to have left the area around 1850, when they sold their property to the Flynns who lived there for the remainder of the century. A little lake situated up the hill near the main residence still bears the name of Flynn (and as an aside to fishermen, is by far the better of the two lakes for speckled and rainbow trout).

There is some question, however, as to who actually settled first in the area in the early part of the nineteenth century. It has been suggested that a Métis family, the Mousseaus, was living there before the Harringtons. Unable to come to any conclusive decision, provincial authorities decided to recognize both families by calling the area Harrington Lake/Lac Mousseau.

The Registry office records now in Maniwaki, Quebec, show that in 1902, two half-brothers from Michigan, W.A. Drum and W.L. Donnelly, bought property around the lake and built a sawmill there. A few years later, they sold their interest to Roger W. Robertson of Carleton Place, Ontario, near Ottawa, who sold it, in turn, to W.C. Edwards and Company Limited in 1911. Later, the company sold the property to W.C. Edwards himself.

Upon W.C. Edwards's death in 1921, part of the lake property was sold to his nephew, Lieutenant-Colonel Cameron Macpherson Edwards. Lieutenant-Colonel Edwards had been born on September 28, 1881 in North Nation Mills, Quebec, about thirty miles southeast of Ottawa. Like many members of his family, he had a strong sense of public duty, and served in the military for a number of years. During World War I, he raised and commanded the 28th Battalion of Infantry (Ottawa Regiment) in Bermuda and France, and was later transferred to Canadian headquarters in London, England. Wounded in action and mentioned in Dispatches, he was awarded the French Medal of Honour and two bars to the Distinguished Service Order.

An aerial view of Harrington Lake. Below and to the left of the main residence is the change house. To the right of the main residence, beside the lake, is the boathouse, complete with sauna, shower and sleeping quarters.

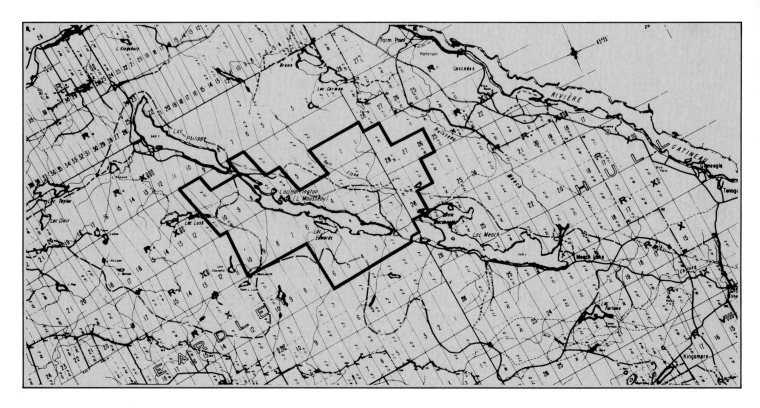

A map of the Harrington Lake-Lac Mousseau region. The enclosed section is all the property owned by Mr. Herridge and Mr. Edwards before the sale to the government in 1950.

He had also been involved for many years in his family's lumber business, W.C. Edwards and Company. This company had originally purchased property on Harrington Lake in order to operate a sawmill there as part of its overall lumbering enterprise. But by the mid-1920's, the lumber business was declining, so Lieutenant-Colonel Edwards removed all the remaining outbuildings connected to the lumber mill operation at Harrington Lake, and built instead the residence which now serves as the Prime Minister's country home.

As well as being involved in the lumber business, the Edwards family was also very active in the development of agriculture in and around the Ottawa Valley area. Lieutenant-Colonel Edwards spent a good deal of money developing part of the Harrington Lake area into a working farm. Judging from available records, however, it does not appear to have been a self-supporting project. Before the land was sold to the federal government in 1951, there were a number of buildings on the property reflecting this interest in agriculture, including a farmhouse, a pump house, a hay barn, a carriage shed, a dairy and an ice house. All have since been demolished.

By 1925, the approximately five thousand acres of land around Harrington Lake had been purchased by two men – Lieutenant-Colonel Edwards, who owned about two-thirds of the property, and the Honourable William Duncan Herridge.

Only one other family, the Healeys, retained a lot near the lake until 1951, when they sold it to the federal government. In 1955 Stanley Healey became caretaker of the entire Harrington Lake property. He was one of the eight Healey children whose grandfather, Edward Healey, had built the original log house near the lake in the 1840's. He spent his whole life in the woods around the lake, enjoying the hardworking life of a naturalist. During the winter he would walk through the fields with pockets full of apples and grain for the animals. Even today, as if expecting to meet him, the deer come right up to the house to look for food.

Like his fellow property owner, William Herridge was very much involved in public life. Six years after his first wife died in 1925, he married Mildred Bennett, the sister of R.B. Bennett, Prime Minister of Canada at that time. That same year, Mr. Herridge was named Minister to Washington and remained Canada's diplomatic representative to the United States until the return of the Liberal government in 1935.

Mr. Herridge's son William now lives in Toronto with his wife and family, and was most helpful to me in my research on Harrington Lake. He mentioned that most of Prime Minister Bennett's "New Deal" speeches had been drafted by his father and Mr. Rod Finlayson in the boathouse below the guest cottage. From his description, I can almost picture them sitting there, with the lake waters lapping quietly beneath them, a handful of men in complete solitude, seeking a way to deliver the nation from a great economic depresssion.

When Mr. Herridge moved back to Canada from Washington, he returned to the log house near the lake, which was to serve as his home until 1956. His wife Mildred had died in 1938, and he spent his remaining years at the guest cottage, which the Herridge family referred to as the "House on the Hill", during the summer, or at the log cabin about a mile away during the winter months.

By 1951, the federal government had purchased all the property around Harrington Lake. This consisted of the Edwards-Herridge property and the small plot of land owned by the Healey family. During the next six years, the residence at Harrington Lake was rented seasonally on a first-come-first-served basis, and because few repairs were carried out during these years, the property and buildings became increasingly rundown.

When the government purchased the property and buildings owned by Mr. Edwards and Mr. Herridge in 1951, a special deed was signed with Mr. Herridge, which gave him the right to use and live in the three dwellings he had built on his property for as long as he lived. Following his death in 1961, the summer cottage near the west end of the lake, the boathouse below it, and the winterized log cabin about a mile away, reverted to the Crown. The summer cottage and the boathouse are now used by the family and friends of the Prime Minister. The log cabin has been gutted and remodeled for use as a stop station for cross-country skiers using National Capital Commission trails through this part of the Gatineau Hills. In fact, skiers who use trails in these parts may pass two stately pillars in the middle of the woods, which mark the entrance to the former country home of the Honourable William D. Herridge.

From Government Property . . .

In 1945, the federal government retained the services of the eminent French city planner, Jacques Gréber, to prepare a long-range master plan to develop the 900-square-mile region surrounding the national capital. Tabled in Parliament on May 22, 1951, the report included many suggestions for the development of this area, among them a recommendation that a hotel resort complex similar to the one at Lake Louise, Alberta be built at Harrington Lake.

The park area north of Ottawa, which the government had been enlarging by continued expropriation, seemed to have excellent potential for tourism and local governments and elected federal members were eager to support any move that would bring much needed money to their local treasuries. The endorsement of this recommendation for Harrington Lake by a majority of the Joint Senate and House Committee on the Federal District Commission appeared to seal the fate of this lovely part of western Quebec.

But not everyone wanted this wilderness haven changed into a centre for tourism. Among the opponents of the idea was Major-General Howard Kennedy, the Chairman of the Federal District Commission. Convinced that the park should remain as untouched and natural as possible, the Chairman set his mind on devising a plan of how best to use the Harrington Lake property in a public way – but without the presence of the public. He came up with the idea to use the property as a country retreat for the Prime Minister. The election of the Right Honourable John G. Diefenbaker's government in 1958 provided him with just the opportunity he needed to implement such a plan.

. . . To The Prime Minister's Country Home

Until 1957, all Canadian Prime Ministers, with the exception of the Right Honourable R.B. Bennett, had been from central Canada. Politics was a gentleman's game, seen not as a responsibility for the largest economic and most complex political and social undertaking in the country, but rather as a cause to which persons of affluence and position could lend their support as part of their established family duty to their community and to their country. Most had homes away from Ottawa where their families stayed. When in Ottawa, politicians lived at one of the prestigious old apartment hotels – the Roxborough, for instance – returning to their own homes and summer residences as soon as the House prorogued each spring.

John Diefenbaker was the first real exception to this rule. After his first major electoral victory, he moved from Saskatchewan to Ottawa and consequently had no summer or country place to which he could easily retreat. After an active year as Prime Minister leading a minority government, he appreciated more than anyone the importance of a place where he and his wife could get away from the rigours and demands of the highest political office in the country. By this time, the houses and lands at Harrington Lake were already owned by the federal government. But John Diefenbaker needed some convincing before he would accept Major-General Kennedy's proposal. Because Mr. Diefenbaker was an avid fisherman, the best way to persuade him seemed to be by showing him what a good spot Harrington Lake was for trout fishing. And so Stanley Healey, the caretaker, was instructed to take Mr. Diefenbaker fishing. "And," Mr. Healey recalls, "I was to be sure Mr. Diefenbaker caught a trout."

Catch a trout he did, and on June 16, 1959, Harrington Lake became the official country residence for future Canadian Prime Ministers.

The pace of life in the late 1950's was dramatically different from that faced by Prime Ministers twenty years later. Mr. Healey mentioned one weekend in the early 1960's when, faced with a threat on his life, Mr. Diefenbaker had been surrounded by RCMP officers while staying at Harrington Lake. After enduring their presence for a whole day, Mrs. Diefenbaker is said to have advised them to return to Ottawa, assuring them all that there was little danger. For more than a decade now, however, there has been continuous surveillance of the house at Harrington Lake.

People can live with the loss of privacy. But I, for one, am not sure I will ever be able to live with the knowledge that my loved ones are never secure.

Prime Minister Diefenbaker and Happy fishing for trout at Harrington Lake.

Prime Minister Diefenbaker oversees the hitching of a dog team. 1962.

Mrs. Diefenbaker, getting ready to skate on the frozen lake, laces her skates on the steps of the change house. 1962.

*Prime Minister Pearson and President
Lyndon B. Johnson take time out from talks
on Canadian-American relations to pose for
photographers at Harrington Lake.*

A Tour of Harrington Lake

THE EXTERIOR

The main residence where the Prime Minister and his family actually stay is one of four buildings on the southeast end of the lake. A short distance from the main house at the bottom of the hill on the lake is a boathouse, complete with a bedroom, a shower and sauna, where the stouthearted can relax and later enjoy a swim in the cold lake nearby. A motorboat and two rowboats are moored at the docks near the sandy beach about 150 feet away, and I can remember with pleasure many hours spent canoeing the four miles to the other end of the lake.

A third building located about half-a-mile north of the Prime Minister's main country residence serves as the caretaker's house. The original home of the Gillespie family, this log building, dating from approximately 1850, was moved in 1921 from the main entrance gate at the end of the Meach Lake road to its present site on the edge of the forest. Since then, all subsequent caretakers have lived there. When the federal government purchased the O'Brien cottage, a huge castle-like house on the edge of a cliff overlooking Meach Lake, Cabinet meetings which had formerly been held at Harrington Lake were held at the cottage instead. Mr. and Mrs. Lionel Desjardins, who are employed by the Department of Public Works to keep the buildings at the lake cleaned and repaired, now live in a part of the O'Brien cottage all year round.

The barn beside the old Gillespie house was originally built in 1929 under the auspices of Lieutenant-Colonel Edwards, as an experiment in prefabricated concrete post and panel structures. The original plan had been to market the product extensively throughout Ontario and Quebec as a less expensive and more convenient structure for the storage of grains and the housing of livestock. That barn is now in need of repair, and is rarely used except as a temporary shelter for dogs and horses.

The house that Cameron Macpherson Edwards built at Harrington Lake in the 1920's was typical of the country residences of the well-to-do during the first quarter of the twentieth century – a true country mansion on a hill. Distinguished by two large fieldstone chimneys in the living and dining room areas, the two-storey frame structure is covered with wood originally cut in the Edward's mill nearby, now painted white with blue trim.

THE FIRST FLOOR

Surrounded by perfectly manicured lawns, hedges and trees, the house has no less than ten bedrooms and six bathrooms. To prevent it from falling into serious disrepair, it was modernized and completely overhauled during the Pearsons' stay there, and is now fully equipped – it even has two dishwashers, three refrigerators and most of the other luxuries of a modern home.

In contrast, early Canadian furnishings, including hooked rag rugs and pine furniture, add a very rugged and rustic look to the interior of the house, and a mood of calm informality is felt immediately by everyone who enters this country home.

Through the main door off a large veranda, where metal chimes catch the slightest breeze, a visitor to Harrington Lake enters a small hall with a deep cloakroom and dark hardwood floors. Paintings and family photographs line the walls in the hall to the left, which leads to a bathroom, two bedrooms and a combination laundry and storage room.

To the immediate right of this foyer is the living room. It is comfortable in the same way as the old, tattered wool sweaters we have all on occasion been admonished for wearing in public. Everyone who has ever used this room has felt perfectly at home there. Budgetary and other financial commitments kept me from repairing and redecorating some of the older and more dowdy-looking pieces of furniture in that room, but in retrospect, I think that the lived-in look that prevailed was one of the house's essential charms.

In any of the homes in which we have lived, I have always sought to achieve a combination of comfort and elegance. Thanks to the professional advice and creative ability of Cecilia Humphreys and her sister, Maureen F. Lonergan, I have learned during the past few years how to transform any house interior into a delightful and co-ordinated whole.

Harrington Lake was no exception to their rule that the entire house must be considered when decorating, rather than one room at a time. A house must have a theme – a feeling that is at its heart, a statement of the character of the people who live there. But such attempts to tame a house, to change or impose one's will upon it, must also take into account its architecture and its history.

In this respect, Harrington Lake presented us with a very special challenge. For from the first day we arrived there, it was obvious that this particular house, in this majestic setting had certain features and qualities that were a permanent and essential part of its character. From the vastness of the lake and the forest, to the isolation and ruggedness of the terrain, this was a very special place.

The house had a history, with so many stories to tell. It almost seemed to warn those who would call it home, "Do not try to change me too much; for unlike temporary residents over the years, I have withstood the test of time."

*The dining room at Harrington Lake is
dominated by a huge fieldstone fireplace and
furnished in early Canadian pine.*

Catherine Clark playing in the living room
with her cousins, Gordon, Todd and John
Zubyck.

But let's return to the present. One of the dominant features of the living room is the massive fieldstone fireplace that fills a third of the wall on the southwest end of the house. Behind one of the framed pictures on the mantle you can sometimes see Mickey, a little grey mouse, eating a piece of fruit or raisins from a pottery bowl.

Mickey the mouse was no more than six inches long, but managed for almost two months to frustrate all my attempts to capture him. It is almost embarrassing to admit to having played games with a mouse, but anyone who has ever been plagued by the presence of mice in the house will appreciate my efforts. Traps, cheese, cookies and cats all proved useless. And so, after a while, I gave up, and set out my own terms for a truce. Mickey was not to disturb us when we had company; in return, I would leave food on the mantle for him each night. As is often the case with children, Catherine became quite attached to the idea of a small "pet" in the house, and wanted very much to make him a toque, convinced by all the Christmas stories that Mickey was really Santa Mouse in disguise!

Moving to the left of this huge fireplace you can look out through the two large windows overlooking one of the most beautiful views this country has to offer: a completely pure lake, four miles long and surrounded by acre upon acre of deciduous trees. Temperamental, the lake could be smooth and lazy in early morning, and then black and violent in the afternoon. Lakes have the power to interpret visually Nature's moods, and Harrington's miles of unspoiled beauty, isolated from its sister lakes by both distance and law, were no exception.

I remember being out alone in the canoe one day, paddling along, lost in my thoughts, when suddenly a summer storm began to whip the water all around me. Unable to return to shore, I paddled with the wind toward a small island in the middle of the lake, where I managed to dock and stay until the storm passed. Having worried the whole time that someone might be hurt trying to find and rescue me, I was almost pleased – and definitely humbled – to learn upon my return that no one had even missed me, as my family thought I had been sleeping upstairs.

As we continue past the living room with its glorious view of the lake, we come to an enclosed patio where we used to eat in the summer, weather permitting. I can remember how I used to yearn for a barbecued steak on a hot summer's night, but, afraid of hurting the chef's feelings, would eat whatever he had chosen to prepare instead.

There were times, when that patio was alive with activity, as children charged across the lawn for that perennial summer favourite – barbecued hotdogs.

Prime Minister Clark reading on the patio
at Harrington Lake.

Prime Minister Clark and Ms. McTeer enjoy a kitchen chat with Ms. McTeer's sister and brother-in-law, Colleen and Gordon Zubyck.

We always try to keep one weekend in July open for family and friends. For the two chosen days in 1979, the sun shone, the fish bit, and only one child had to be rushed off to the city with a broken tooth suffered during a friendly baseball game. Even that sobering experience was turned into high adventure. Today, the child still proudly displays the gap in his mouth under his new tooth, recounting to his friends how he had been rushed in a police car from Harrington to the dentist's office. The members of the RCMP who serve as security for the Prime Minister and his family are very sensitive to the needs and fears of young children. I will never forget that in order to calm this little boy, they allowed him to turn on the flashing light and to speak in code over their car radio to advise those of us who had stayed at the lake that he was going to be all right.

The dining room at Harrington is identical to the living room, lacking only the splendid view. The same large fieldstone fireplace stands directly opposite the one in the living room, and in the winter, after an afternoon of skating or cross-country skiing, I remember candlelight dinners and animated conversation at small tables, where family and friends alike basked in the glowing warmth of these two immense fireplaces.

Anyone who grew up in the country, used to the size and purpose of the farm kitchen, would appreciate this part of the house at Harrington Lake. There are two doors in the kitchen. One leads to the summer kitchen, where just outside the sheets are hung to dry and absorb that fresh, outdoor scent that all the cleaning potions on the market cannot duplicate. The second one leads to a two-car garage where we stored all the wood for the fireplace, our skis and our riding tack.

The kitchen itself is bright and spacious. During our stay, its wooden panels were painted a high-gloss white, and there was ample cupboard space for all our household needs. The room was fully equipped with an electric stove, a refrigerator, and a dishwasher. A movable wooden cutting board was set near the stove at one end of the room. It was here that Catherine and I would make our edible treasures early on summer mornings. A teak dining room set with chair cushions in green plaid tweed was placed at the other end of the room where friends could gather to drink coffee and talk while I carried on preparing the meal.

No matter how hard I tried to keep them out, our guests would gravitate toward the kitchen whenever we had a party at the lake. It was almost as if standing against the counter or leaning against the fridge offered some feeling of comfort and informality to all those who were there.

The screen door leading to the summer kitchen was broken when we arrived, and during our stay, a fat and bold racoon used to try daily to come in and join us for lunch. When I remembered to lock this door, the old racoon would create a terrible scene banging on the screen with his paws, and leaving only at the sight of the broom aimed in his direction.

But the kitchen at the lake is memorable to me for more than its potential invaders. Cooking is one of the most relaxing activities I know. When I was a child, we all had our assigned tasks. In addition to feeding my pony, my task was to make the meals for our family before our mother would return from work in the evening. On weekends, my father would banish us all from the kitchen, in order to allow him to create one of his exotic dishes to try out on his six eager guinea pigs. We loved it when he cooked these unusual delicacies just for our pleasure. We must be very special, we used to think, for our father to cook such fancy meals for us. But during the week, when he was away, the chore of cooking fell to me.

Up at the lake, miles from the chef who ruled the kitchen at 24 Sussex, I could again putter around my own kitchen, preparing the foods I wanted in my own way and in my own time. All the foods I had a yearning to eat – Italian dishes, relishes, pastries and cakes – I made in that kitchen. And odd as it may sound, the time I spent stirring and kneading and tasting in that big, old farm kitchen had almost a therapeutic effect on me. It gently gave me back my perspective on the reality of my life at that time.

THE SECOND FLOOR

Excluding the basement, the house at Harrington Lake has only two storeys. Yet the second storey alone, with its eight bedrooms and four bathrooms, is bigger than many people's entire houses.

The carpeted stairs off the front hall lead straight to the upstairs landing where, during our stay there, I had placed one of the beautiful porcelain dolls my husband had brought home for me from his trip to Japan in 1979. My sister, Patricia, had made a large woven hanging of a sunrise, which was placed at the top of the stairs to complement the exterior view seen through a window nearby. Photographs of the ranching country of southern Alberta, taken over a number of years by Joe's father, Charles, were hung all along the wall to form a collage of framed colour against the white interior wooden siding. The large carved banister, with sufficient splinters in it to discourage even the most rambunctious child from sliding down it, was decorated at Christmas with a twelve-foot-long garland of Victoria holly, tied in place with red velvet ribbons.

The master bedroom on the second floor, which is surrounded by windows on three sides, overlooks the lake below. In the spring, one can fall asleep to the sound of rushing water over the little dam nearby, where the Edwards's sawmill once prepared lumber for shipment to Europe.

Prime Minister Clark, Ms. McTeer and Catherine enjoy some tobogganing over Christmas, 1979.

*A child's bedroom on the second floor of
Harrington Lake during the stay of Prime
Minister Clark and his family.*

*The master bedroom on the second floor at
Harrington Lake, with windows overlooking
the lake. 1980.*

I can remember unpacking clothes one day in that master bedroom, and coming across a yellow telephone high up on a shelf in the closet. "The colour is fine," I thought, "but the location will never do." Making a mental note to have it moved into Joe's study, I went about my business, until the following day when the RCMP asked if it would be convenient for them to "check the phone".

"They are all working well," I assured the poor man, who must have wondered at my insistence. "It is the one upstairs," he said, "The one in the master bedroom. The one that can be used by the Prime Minister in case of war. The yellow one in the closet."

All that night I was unable to sleep. And as I lay there, I thought of the incongruities of life. Or maybe it was the price of our particular life that bothered me: the knowledge that to live in this house, to feel the peace that it gave us, we had also to accept the reality of yellow telephones.

Harrington Lake was one of the consolations of such a life. Not only was it beautiful, but the feeling was restful. Stanley Healey told me once that all those who had lived there sought to return. The place cast a magical spell that touched everyone who had come to know and love it. "They all would return," he said, "and they all wept when they had to leave."

Harrington Lake – the house and the place – was the greatest source of privacy and peace that was offered me when my husband was Prime Minister. Perhaps it was too much of a cocoon, too much of a place "far from the madding crowd." But it helped to keep me whole; helped me to meet all the responsibilities that were important and crucial to my daily life at that time. It was my home. And somehow, I will forever be grateful to that unknowing trout on the end of Mr. Diefenbaker's fishing line.

Prime Minister Clark working at
Harrington Lake.

Prime Minister Clark, Ms. McTeer and Catherine strolling down the lane on their way to the main road at Harrington Lake. Spring, 1980.

The author and publisher would like to thank the following for providing illustrations for this book.

Ted Grant: pp. 41, 45, 46, 47, 49, 59, 64, 65, 66 (l.), 67, 68, 69, 70, 71 (u.), 72, 85, 92, 93, 96, 98, 99, 102, 103, 104 120, 121, 123, 124, 127, 128, 129, 131, 132. Public Archives of Canada: p. 12, PC-801232; p. 13, PR-501332; p. 15, PA-123534; p. 19, PA-125907; p. 21, PR-125238; p. 24, PR-125912; p. 31, PR-128112; p. 33, PR-128116; p. 34, PR-125910; p. 38, PA-128107; p. 88, PR-129346; p. 89, PA-129349; p. 117, 11034-3-10A. Clive Webster, NFB: pp. 42, 56, 66 (u.). Andrew Newton: pp. 16, 28, 29. Scott Grant, pp. 11, 71 (l.). Carolyn Weir: pp. 115, 116. The Deifenbaker Centre: p. 114. Ottawa Archives: p. 9, CA1795. Mia & Klaus: p. 105. Page 57: by permission of The Prime Minister's Office. Pages 43, 45: Courtesy of *Chatelaine Magazine*. Pages 75, 76, 77: from the private collection of the Major family. Page 79: from the private collection of the Perley-Robertson family. Pages 81, 82, 83: from the private collection of Mrs. Martine Feaver.

Every reasonable effort has been made to find copyright holders of the photographs and illustrations. The publishers would be pleased to have any errors or omissions brought to their attention.

Index